THE STOUR VALLEY PATH

BY

EDWARD R GRIFFITHS

A JOURNEY TO THE SOURCE OF A FINE ENGLISH RIVER,
IN EASY STAGES WITH GUIDE MAPS AND ANECDOTES

x...towards the main road at the bottom of the hill
(Durweston)....Day 3 Stage 5 Bryanston to Durweston

First published 1994

ⓒ Edward R Griffiths

ISBN No 0 9519376 1 8

Published by Green Fields Books,
13 Dalewood Avenue, Bear Cross,
Bournemouth, BH11 9NR

Printed by Brown & Son, Crowe Arch Lane, Ringwood, Hants. Tel: (0425) 476133

CONTENTS

ROUTE MAP

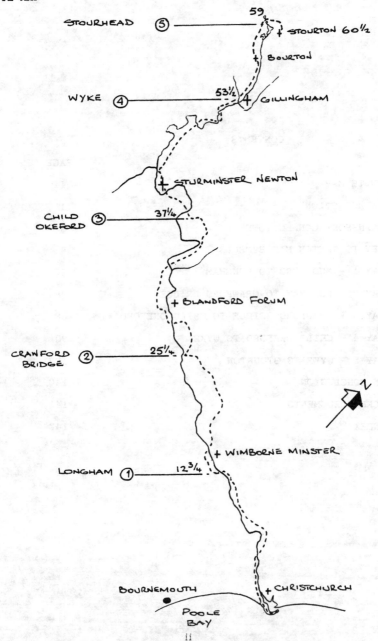

STOURHEAD ⑤ —————————— 59
                        + STOURTON 60½
                     + BOURTON

WYKE ④ ——————— 53½ + GILLINGHAM

                + STURMINSTER NEWTON

CHILD OKEFORD ③ ——— 37¼

                + BLANDFORD FORUM

CRANFORD BRIDGE ② ——— 25¼

                + WIMBORNE MINSTER

LONGHAM ① ——— 12¾

N

BOURNEMOUTH   + CHRISTCHURCH
POOLE BAY

ii

THE STOUR VALLEY PATH

INTRODUCTION

The search for the source of the Wiltshire and Dorset Stour may not compare on a global scale with journeys to the sources of such world-famous rivers as the Nile or the Amazon but this adventure is not without distinct similarities.

There is no documentary evidence that the River Stour has ever been explored (before now) from sea to source as one single undertaking, so who is to say that this is not a legitimate journey of discovery in which new ground is broken and dark secrets are revealed in the depths of Central Southern England?

Believe me, this is not a journey for the faint-hearted, even if excursions to high ground are usually optional and the route can be covered by any walker of average ability. No, the dangers of which I speak are real enough. Unless you undertake this venture in dry weather, you may encounter quagmire and floods of biblical proportions - well, maybe not that bad although you should wear waterproofed walking boots as some of the farmland is practically at River level and takes some time to dry out after prolonged periods of rain - and this IS England. You will meet wild animals. In a two-day period, and on official footpaths between Blandford Forum and Marnhull, I went through three fields which harboured quite large bulls - but they were being kept quite busy by the requisite number of cows at the time.

Furthermore, although this, presumably, will not be a natural consequence of undertaking this voyage, my bus between Blandford and Marnhull was attacked by a young lady wielding a Volkswagen Golf. Eventful area, isn't it?

However, I doubt that explorers in darkest Africa had to contend with such dangers as these (except the mud, perhaps) - so, when you have completed the distance from Christchurch Harbour entrance to Six Wells Bottom, you will be able to count yourself among "The Few".

Now, having seen off the less dedicated and adventurous readers, let's have a look at the manifold reasons for making this journey at all.

The River Stour has played host to many peoples over thousands of years, providing water, fish, wonderful grazing land and perfect arable conditions on its flood plains. Cereals and cattle alike have grown fat and succulent on the lush, silt-enriched land and, before it was safe enough to actually live on the edge of the River, Bronze Age, Iron Age, Roman and Norman settlements were established on high vantage points within close walking distance of its banks. We shall pass by, through or over many such sites and more details will be given in the text as you approach them but, for now, a short list will be sufficient to whet your appetite. Right at the start of the Walk we go over Hengistbury Head, followed by Dudsbury Camp, Cowgrove Roman Road, Badbury Rings, Shapwick Roman Road, Hod Hill and Hambledon Hill.

Many religious orders were established along the accommodating banks of the Stour, some having disappeared whilst others have merged into the villages which sprang up alongside them to provide them with labour and services. Indeed, this journey gives us ample opportunity to enjoy many delightful churches of all ages and to share in the peace and tranquility of their settings. We pass close by many of them but several more are included where they are of particular interest and worth a short diversion.

Other communities were established alongside the fords and bridges across the River as travellers focusing on these few crossings brought more and more custom to the convenient inns and stables. Such providers of rest and sustenance were to be found in villages such as Iford, Canford, Tarrant Crawford (by the Abbey), Fiddleford, Sturminster Newton and Gillingham whilst innumerable flour mills were established on the Stour to provide bread for the thriving communities along the River from source to sea. Many of these mills survive to this day and our route gives us ample opportunity to visit and to see some of them still working whilst others have either disappeared completely, are in disrepair or have been converted into living accommodation.

Notwithstanding these considerations, the River Stour runs through some of the most beautiful pastoral scenery in the whole country - a fact acknowledged by the National Trust who have acquired several estates, individual buildings and hill forts along the way, none of which pass without comment in the narrative.

Now, to settle the query which is bound to be raised by many who will be contemplating this Walk. Why walk from sea to source and not the other way? This can be answered in two ways - one philosophical and the other practical.

Firstly, in the age old tradition of such journeys of discovery, we are searching for the source, not the termination, of the River. Discoveries of strange lands were always made by seaward arrival (by British explorers, anyway) and further exploration was always, therefore, from the sea inwards. The second, purely practical, reason is that our route runs from South to North thus ensuring that the prevailing wind will normally be coming from over our left shoulder and not into our face. Similarly, we will also be walking away from the sun, ensuring that our view of the country ahead of us will be enhanced by the sunlight and not dimmed by the sun shining into our eyes.

Starting at the entrance to Christchurch Harbour at Mudeford,
we leave the conurbation of Christchurch/Bournemouth behind us
on the very first day and, from then on, we will be cossetted
by the peace and warmth of the pastoral life. (If you happen
to be a farmer, I mean of course the layman's ideal of the
peace and warmth of pastoral life).

On this Walk, there exist several opportunities to cheat - I
mean, to revise the route to suit your own particular
preferences or to avoid your own particular dislikes . For
instance, if you can't bear the bustle and claustrophobia of
towns and urban fringes, you can take a bus straight out of
Christchurch towards Wimborne and, at several points along the
rest of the journey, you will find that many bus routes
approximate to our path.

However, Hengistbury Head is particularly fine and the River
plain walk from Holdenhurst to Longham (both on the fringes of
Bournemouth) is full of interest so, in order to be able to
claim that you have walked the length of the River Stour, a
little urbanization should be tolerated on Day 1.

The rest is pure magic so, on a pleasantly dry and sunny day,
set off from Mudeford spit in keen anticipation of the
delights ahead that are, for the want of a better
all-embracing phrase, - pure England.

Oh, by the way, this being England, a few strange facts and
myths, legends and ghostly happenings have been included in
the Stage narratives. However, if you are of a nervous
disposition, you can always gloss over them.

Anyway, have a good look at the bus timetables. The Wilts
and Dorset red timetable will cover the main routes but, for
the rural services, you should get hold of a copy of "Public
Transport in Rural Dorset" published by Dorset County Council
and available free from most Tourist Information Centres in
the area or direct from County Hall, Dorchester. The Stage
maps on each day are highly detailed but not to scale. If
you want scale, you should consult Ordnance Survey Landranger
Series maps Nos 195, 194 and 183 in that order. You should
have these maps, anyway. The sketch maps only cover
distances of a few yards either side of our route so, if you
do happen to wander off to view something that has caught your
eye - or even gone wrong - you will need the OS map to find
your way back.

Just a few more words before you throw your rucksack over your
shoulder and depart for pastures new. Firstly, remember
"The Country Code". I know you don't need me to remind you
that, if you find a gate open, leave it open but otherwise you
should always close gates behind you. We are only visitors
in the countryside, especially in arable and pasture land.
Take care of it, don't drop litter and respect the privacy of
those whose cottage doorways you go past. Appreciation is

one thing, intrusion is another.

Beyond that, some of the rules and/or guidelines concerning Rights of Way may not be generally known and could bear highlighting here.

Signposting and Waymarking:
The County Council only has a duty to erect and maintain signposts where a public Right of Way actually leaves a metalled (tarmac) road. Additionally, the County Council has the power to Waymark paths where the route is not obvious - but it is not obliged to do so.
Stiles and gates have to be maintained by the landowner where they cross footpaths -"to the standard of repair required to prevent unreasonable interference with the rights of the persons using the footpath or bridleway" - Section 28:Countryside Act 1968.

Path through fields:
Under the Rights of Way Act 1990, if a path follows the edge of a field, the surface must not be ploughed or disturbed. The law requires a minimum width of 1.5m for a footpath and 2.5m for a bridleway at the edge of a field.
If a path crosses a field or enclosure, the path must be reinstated within 14 days of ploughing to a minimum width of 1m for a footpath and 2m for a bridleway.

Obstruction or loss of path:
The County Council recommends that, when faced with an obstruction on the correct route i.e. lack of stiles, gates or exits from fields, make a slight deviation and report the obstruction to the Footpaths Liaison Officer of the Parish in which the obstruction occurs or to the Rights of Way Section of the County Council - they are always keen to help. Further, such obstructions are illegal under Section 137 of the 1980 Highways Act.

By the way - under Section 59 of the Wildlife and Countryside Act 1981, a bull may not be released into a field or enclosure crossed by a Right of Way unless it is less than 10 months old or, if older, accompanied by cows or heifers (apparently, but not officially, 11 cows is the minimum safe number of cows per bull or it may still have the energy to chase you).

Now, wearing the recommended boots and carrying enough waterproofs to be prepared for the vagaries of the English weather, it's time to start at last, so go out and thoroughly enjoy yourself.

Lastly, the journey is divided into 5 approximately 12 miles long sections (adjusted to suit bus routes and accommodation possibilities) so that the whole journey can be undertaken in one week, but it can also be treated as 5 separate journeys to be enjoyed over any length of time, perhaps to be shared between the seasons or as day trips.

The section on "Transport Connections" indicates where cars can stop either to drop you off or to stay all day awaiting your return by bus - or to stay near a morning bus stop so that you can walk back to the car (my own preferred system). Just let me make this plea - When parking the car, make sure that you don't block anybody's access or cause a hazard in a country lane and, don't assume that pub car parks are for general use. They are for customers so, even if you intend to have the most expensive meal available when you return in the evening, ask the landlord's permission before you abandon your car in his private car park.

All bus routes which are closely approached during each Stage are also shown so that you can break a Stage at any time before the official Day's end.

Finally, a few days before the 1st printing of this guide, I found that Dorset County Council and Greenlink had been preparing 'The Stour Valley Way'- a route from Hengistbury Head which finishes at Sturminster Marshall. This will be Waymarked by June 1994 and the accompanying leaflet will be available by the Summer of 1995 from Tourist Information or D.C.C. outlets. Dorset County Council will be continuing the route from Sturminster Marshall northwards.

Following discussions with Richard Hands of Greenlink, we both decided to leave our respective routes unchanged whilst mutually acknowledged. In fact, I have to warn you that, if you are following this "Stour Valley Path" guided route, don't be diverted from our route by the 'Stour Valley Way' signs and markers or you will miss some of the delights that I have found for you. On the other hand, feel free to wander off whenever you wish if the leaflet entices you elsewhere.

...a convenient bench and the Church
of St Paul, Hammoon - Day 4, Stage 2

THE STOUR VALLEY PATH - TRANSPORT CONNECTIONS

	STAGE MILES	CAR STOP	BUS STOPS
DAY 1			
STAGE 1	2	Hengistbury Head - Terminal	-
2	3.25	Wick Car Park	90a at Tuckton
3	4.75	Iford Lane area	7 buses at Iford
4	4.75	- ditto -	- ditto -
	5.25	Riverside Avenue	165 Castle Lane
5	6	Holdenhurst side of F/Bridge	165 Yeomans Way
6	7.50	Throop Mill	-
8	11	Parley Cross	Choice of 5 plus 134 at Dudsbury
9	12.75	Longham Lay-By	X1 and 135 on Rt
DAY 2			
STAGE 1	0	Longham Lay-By	X1 and 135
2	1.50	Hampreston Village	-
	1.75	Stapehill Road Lay-By	-
4	2.75	Fox Lane	90 By-Pass R/bt.
5	3.75	Canford Magna	139
6	5	Merley Ways	X13,90 and 132
7	6.50	Merley Ways	X13, 139 By-Pass
8	7	Eye Bridge Car Park	320 Cowgrove FRI
9	8.75	Bridleway Car Park	-
10	9.50	Bridleway End	-
11	11.50	Shapwick	320 Shapwick FRI
	12.50	Crawford Bridge	X13,139 Spetis'y

	STAGE MILES	CAR STOP	BUS STOP
DAY 3			
STAGE 1	0	Crawford Bridge	X13,139 Spetis'y
	1.75	Tarrant Keynston nr Church	182 THUR and SAT
2	3.50	Charlton Marshall Lay-By	X13,139
3	5.75	Blandford St Mary	X13,139 in town
4	6.75	- ditto -	111 Bryanston PO
5	8.25	Durweston Village	X13,X94,139 etc.
6	8.75	Stourpaine	139,X13,X38 & 47
7	9.50	Hod Hill Lay-By	X13,139 on A350
	11	By Road - Child Okeford	303 to Sturm'ter or Blandford
	12.25	By Hill - Child Okeford	- ditto -
DAY 4			
STAGE 1	0	Child Okeford	303 - as above
	1.50	Haywards Bridge Pull-In	X94,303 Sh'stone
2	3.25	Hammoon	190,303 Fid'ford
3	4.75	Fiddleford Manor	- ditto -
	5.75	Sturminster Newton Car Park	X94,303,109,117
4	7	Hinton St Mary	15,109,117,190
5	7	Hinton St Mary	- ditto -
6	10	Marnhull Car Park	- ditto -
7/7a	11.25	Fifehead Magdalen	46 and 48
	12.75	West Stour	46,48,242
8	12.75	West Stour	- ditto -
9	16.25	Wyke Crossroads	46,47 or 109,117 in Gillingham

STAGE MILES		CAR STOP	BUS STOP
DAY 5			
STAGE 1	0	Wyke Crossroads	46,47 or 109,117 in Gillingham
	1	Milton On Stour	30,59,109 & 117
2	2	Silton	109
3	3.25	Bourton	30,59,109 & 117
	4	Pen Mill	-
4	4.50	Harcourt Farm Hairpin	-
	4.75	Bonham	30,59,109,117 at Zeals 1.5 miles
5	5.50	Stourhead Car Park	20,30,59,109,117 at Zeals 2 miles
6	7	- ditto -	20 or as above at Zeals

There may be other alternative buses operating so it will be worth having a good look at your copy of Public Transport in Rural Dorset before setting off. These are issued twice yearly to cover Spring/Summer and Autumn/Winter.

My own preference has been to catch the first available morning bus from a convenient parking point and to walk back to the car during the day. That way, you are not having to rush back for a bus and the day is your own to dawdle and stare if you want to.

KEY TO SKETCH MAP SYMBOLS

ROUTE	- - - - - - -
ROUTE ACROSS OPEN GROUND	-·-·-·-·-·-
HEDGE	
WIRE FENCE	
WOODEN OR IRON FENCE	
STILE	
GATE, LARGE	
GATE, SMALL	
SOLID WALL	
BRIDGE (OVER STREAM)	
DECIDUOUS TREE	
FIR TREE	
HOUSE OR SPECIFIC BUILDING	
VARIOUS BUILDINGS, APPROX	
EMBANKMENT	
OVERHEAD CABLES	—×——×—
RIVER STOUR	
STREAM	
FOOTPATH/BRIDLEWAY SIGN	
ADJOINING SKETCH MAP NO	7/8

DAY 1 - INTRODUCTION

Mudeford to Longham

Starting at the edge of the sea at Christchurch Bay, the South Coast holiday haven, our route takes us to Longham on the outskirts of its more famous neighbour, Bournemouth. On the way, we wander over the Iron Age and Roman settlement of Hengistbury Head, through the Saxon villages of Wick and Holdenhurst and along the riverside after Throop weir. Urban encroachment up to the River edge drives us away a couple of times on this first Stage but, mercifully, only one section has little scenic value and, even here, compensation is offered in the form of a few shops where provisions may be gathered for the rest of the day. After our last spot of urbanization at Parley, we find another hill fort at Dudsbury, now the home of ferocious Girl Guides, and we end the day with a lovely stroll along the edge of the Stour to Longham and the bus home.

	STAGE	MILES	TOTAL
1	Mudeford to Wick Village	2.50	2.50
2	Wick Village to Tuckton	1	3.50
3	Tuckton to Iford	1.25	4.75
4	Iford to Riverside Avenue	1	5.75
5	Riverside Avenue to Throop Old Forge	1.25	7
6	Throop Old Forge to Throop Weir	1	8
7	Throop Weir to Parley Court Pond	1.50	9.50
8	Parley Court Pond to Parley Cross	1.50	11
9	Parley Cross to Longham	1.75	12.75

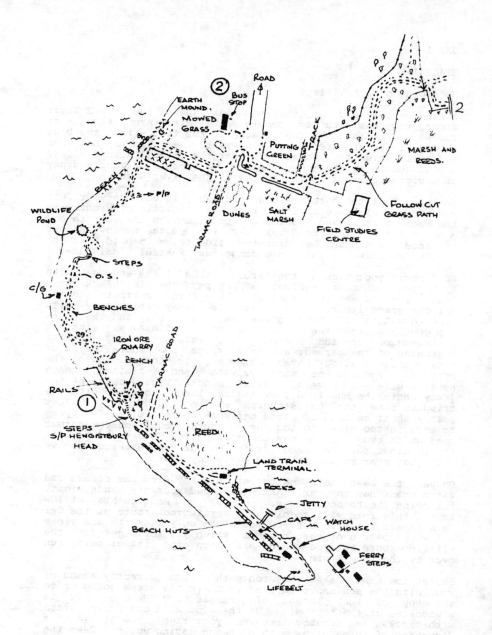

DAY 1 - STAGE 1

DAY 1

STAGE 1

Mudeford to Wick Village

At the extreme end of the sandbank where the tired River
Stour, together with its cousin, the River Avon, flows - or
rushes, depending upon the state of the tide - into the blue
waters of Christchurch Bay, dip your toes into the cool sea
and, retreating to a safer spot near the lifebelt, turn slowly
around and enjoy the moment before you embark on your journey
of exploration to find the source of the River Stour.

Facing out of the harbour, Mudeford Quay is busy on your left
and, in the distance on your right is the Isle of Wight with
the Needles rocks and lighthouse prominent on the Western end
- and all the time, the Rivers race through the narrow harbour
entrance, even when the inrushing tide tries to hold back the
freshwater flow. This is a dangerous, fearful tidal race.

Now, begin your trek on the harbour side of the sandbank with
soft sand underfoot at first as you pass the old, black Watch
House with its warning signs about the strong currents and the
harbour speed limit. At a little stony spit, level with
some work huts, the sand gives way to pebbles and the waves
lap gently against the shore as you continue, enjoying the
soft sounds of the harbour, with distant views of the
beginning of the harbour and the vague spot where the Stour
enters this boating haven somewhere in the region of the
Priory. Passing the many private (and inhabited) beach
huts, a cafe and several toilet blocks, you soon meet the
jetty where the Mudeford Quay ferry lands, together with the
trippers from the Christchurch end of the harbour. Just
past a short section of stone defences where the sea is trying
to edge in too close to the beach huts, you reach the tarmac
road which runs all the way to Hengistbury Head - and here is
the terminus for the Land Train - but keep walking; you've
only just started and it's too early to cheat.

On past the beach huts and toilet blocks, with the creeks and
marsh grass now on your right, the road suddenly bends right,
following the harbour edge. If you want to stay at low
level, this road will rejoin the preferred route at the Car
Park in about 1 mile but you would not only miss the sea views
and views back over the harbour which you would get from the
clifftop route but you would also run the risk of being run
over by the Land Train.

So, at the bend, take the footpath track directly ahead of
you, with the sea shore on your left, to the steps going up to
the top of the plateau of Hengistbury Head. It is
signposted at the bottom. Up the wide wood and gravel steps
with bracken and scrubby trees on your right, you arrive at a
diversion of three paths with a bench facing you. Take the

left of the paths, around the edge of a fence on your left which keeps you away from the cliff edge. From here on, you could wander at will hither and thither over small paths and through the bracken and heather but, being mindful of feathered and scaly residents, we'll keep to the main paths, won't we?

In any event, the views from the clifftop path are superb and we'll be turning inland soon enough.

Just as the fence turns off left, the sea views to the Isle of Purbeck in the distance are extensive, from Ballard Down to Old Harry Rocks, widening as we progress to reveal Corfe Castle and Bournemouth Bay. No, you can't stay at the seaside. You've got the source of a River to find.

Hengistbury Head is the site of a heavily fortified Iron Age port where a vast export/import trade flourished. Here, the Durotriges had settled, having come here from their homelands in North-West Europe. They were highly skilled artisans who traded agricultural implements, coins which were minted right here, metallic ores and pottery for imported European goods.

They were eventually overthrown by the invading 2nd Roman onslaught under Vespasian between AD 45-47. Before then, however, such settlements were often subjected to raids by bandit tribesmen and many Durotrige men and their families left to take shelter in more secure villages under the protection of armed forces and behind massive earthworks. Such strong, defensive works had been necessitated by the earlier invasion by Plautius' troops in AD 43 and our route to the source of the Stour passes close by and over some of these sites such as Badbury Rings, Hod Hill and Hambledon Hill.

All of these forts were eventually overcome by the Vespasian invasion and, by AD 48, the entire West of England was under Roman control - signalling the end of the already customary British way of life (somnolence in the face of technical advancement) and heralding our propulsion into high-tech materialism.

Follow the path, avoiding fenced-off "Cliff Fall" areas, and aim for the distant Coastguard Lookout Station. On the way, you pass an iron-ore quarry on the right which is now a wild-life pond. After this, at the junction of paths, turn left and continue aiming for the CG Station, after which you will reach the OS Survey 36m benchmark plinth. The views on all sides are superb. Follow the narrowing path down the end of the Head and keep straight on after a path joins you from the right. Before another wildlife pond, the track becomes stone-coloured tarmac and, at the pond, you have a clear view on your right of the Avon and the Stour both joining the harbour, through reeds and marshes. In a few yards, the road divides and we take the left fork to the clifftop route whilst the right fork takes the harbourside route. Descending to beach level, notice the reinforcing gambions and groynes attempting to keep the sea away from the cliffs and our path.

Next, we skirt around the LH end of some ancient double-dykes. Past the end of the fenced dykes, the tarmac road ends and the gravel track which replaces it divides near a small earth mound. Take the RH track, parallel to the dykes, with mowed grassland on the left. At the end of the dykes, the harbourside road joins us from the right and goes across our path to the Land Train Terminal and the Rangers Office. Keeping straight on, make your way around the LH end of a grassy mound in front of you and join the tarmac road which leaves the turning circle at the end of the urban road and bears off left to continue on our original line, signposted "Riverside Walk to Wick Village". Continue between the fenced putting green on the left and the grassy mound on the right. At the junction of the Field Studies Centre entrance, the LH track and our path, go straight past the start of the bigger track on the left and go through the kissing gate, signed "Wick Village", in the wooden fence. On open, scrubby grass, keep to the mowed path which meanders between fences on both sides until it terminates at a kissing gate in the far RH corner, near a wide track which goes off left. Through the gate, turn immediately right and follow the fence on your right, behind which are some scrubby bushes and reedy marshes. Follow the fence as it turns left and, if you look back, you can see your starting point clearly defined by the black Watch House at the harbour entrance.

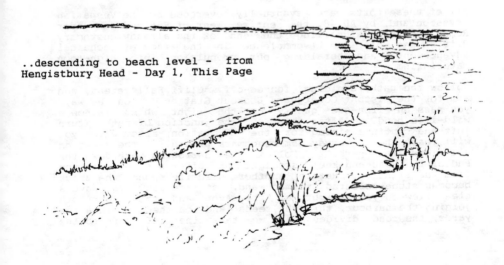

..descending to beach level - from
Hengistbury Head - Day 1, This Page

14

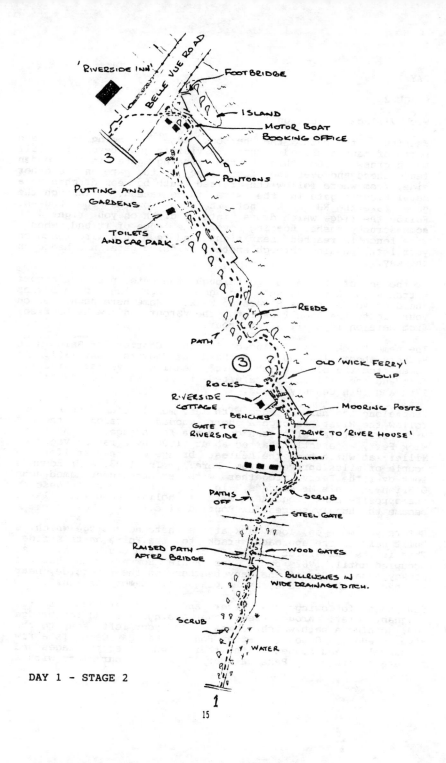

'RIVERSIDE INN'

BELLE VUE ROAD

FOOTBRIDGE

ISLAND

MOTOR BOAT
BOOKING OFFICE

③

PONTOONS

PUTTING AND
GARDENS

TOILETS
AND CAR PARK

REEDS

PATH

③

OLD 'WICK FERRY'
SLIP

ROCKS

RIVERSIDE
COTTAGE

MOORING POSTS

BENCHES

GATE TO
RIVERSIDE

DRIVE TO 'RIVER HOUSE'

PATHS
OFF

SCRUB

STEEL GATE

RAISED PATH
AFTER BRIDGE

WOOD GATES

BULLRUSHES IN
WIDE DRAINAGE DITCH.

SCRUB

WATER

DAY 1 - STAGE 2

1

15

DAY 1

STAGE 2

Wick Village to Tuckton

Keeping to the path, the harbour edge is coming closer and masts of many anchored yachts are visible just beyond the tall marsh grass. Go through the kissing gate in the wooden fence ahead and over the footbridge to the gate on the other side, from where follow the raised path between ditches to a metal kissing gate in the wire fence ahead. Through the gate, take the RH fork, not the one towards the houses. Follow the ridge which drops into a ditch on your right with some scrubby bushes peering over the edge of it and, when a wire fence is reached, bear right and keep this wire fence on your left, passing through another kissing gate in a hedge on the way.

At the end of the fence, go through the gate, past the secure entrance to "River House" and go through the gap in bushes ahead of you onto the Riverside Walk. Somewhere downriver on your right, the Avon runs into the Stour and the harbour so, from here on it's all River Stour.

The name "Wick" was included in the Charters of Baldwin de Redvers about 1100 and of Richard de Redvers about 1161. It comes from the old English "Wic" meaning a village or dairy farm and the village is referred to as "Weeke" or "Week" in 17th and 18th Century deeds.

Keep along the harbour edge with many moorings and benches and follow the River, through a short wooded diversion by the old Wick Ferry gravel slip, and go over a footbridge. The first Wick Ferry apparently started about 1800 by a rather vague Mr Miller, at which time the nearest bridge was that at Iford, a couple of miles upriver from here. In 1903, a Mr Edmunds took over the Ferry, together with a huge rower named John O'Brian. This Mr Edmunds, in 1927, built a boat-house on the opposite bank, together with a holiday camp which later became the hugely successful Pontins site.

Before you move on, look back at the thatched cottage which is built next to the approach track to the Ferry on this side. This is the "Riverside Cottage" of the 18th Century which was occupied until 1982 by a Mrs Annie Bowser with her pet monkey, Anna. One of the many benches on the riverside, near the back of the cottage, has a plaque "In Memory of Anna".

Now keep following the River and skirt around a fairly stagnant inlet, through trees, over a single-railed footbridge and, joining a path which comes from your left, keep to the River's edge. Opposite, after Pontins Holiday Camp, is a row of bungalows and houses with their own river frontages and private moorings. Pass a Car Park on your left with a convenient WC and keep following the delightful river path, past pontoons, a putting green and a small park on the left. Skirt round the Motor Boat Booking Office, a parking area beyond it and several outbuildings until you reach a footbridge on the right which links the main path with a high island between you and the River. Past this footbridge, go up the sloping path onto the pavement in Belle Vue Road. The first bridge across the Stour at this point was built of wood in 1881 and, in order to run trams from Bournemouth to Christchurch, Bournemouth Corporation had to build this new steel bridge. This they accomplished and the first tram passed over it on October 17th 1905. Incidentally, the last tram passed over it on April 8th 1936 and traffic tolls were charged here until 1943.

Now, cross over the road and turn left, away from the River, past the entrance to Riverside Inn and past a bus lay-by.

Keep along the Harbour edge -
Wick Ferry - Day 1, Page 16

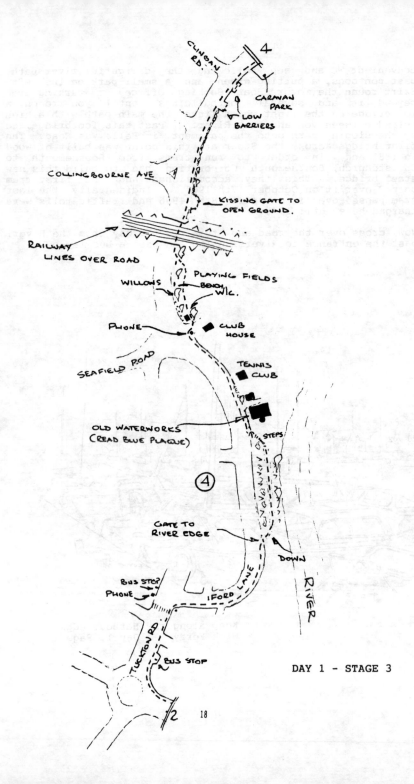

CLINGAN RD.

4

CARAVAN PARK

LOW BARRIERS

COLLINGBOURNE AVE

KISSING GATE TO OPEN GROUND.

RAILWAY LINES OVER ROAD

PLAYING FIELDS

WILLOWS

BENCH W/C.

PHONE

CLUB HOUSE

SEAFIELD ROAD

TENNIS CLUB

OLD WATERWORKS (READ BLUE PLAQUE)

STEPS

④

GATE TO RIVER EDGE

DOWN

RIVER

BUS STOP

PHONE

FORD LANE

FORD

TUCKTON RD.

BUS STOP

DAY 1 - STAGE 3

2

18

DAY 1

STAGE 3

Tuckton to Iford

At the roundabout ahead, turn right into Tuckton Road and go past Riverside Lane to Iford Lane, just after a pedestrian crossing and a Post Office. Turn right into Iford Lane and follow the road round a left hand bend after Riverside Road. As the pavement widens out to a grassy verge, go through a gate in the RH fence and go down a narrow riverside path amongst old trees and parallel to the road. It's only a few hundred yards along here but it gets you away from the road for a while. At the end of the path, go up the steps and rejoin the pavement via a kissing gate at the top.

The smart brick buildings on your right are converted waterworks buildings - note the Blue Plaque commemorating the activities of Count Tchertkov and his friends who printed the first copies of Tolstoy's works right here in this building. About this time, England appears to have had quite a population of Russian emigres.

With houses on high level embankments on the opposite side of the road, keep going along the pavement, past the Southbourne Tennis Club and, after the telephone box, turn into the Playing Fields area but keep following the pavement (It's just that the grass is kinder to your feet, that's all). Past some fine willows and one huge oak tree alongside the road, go under the railway arch and, in 100 yards, go past the kissing gate which leads into the field on your right. The grassy area beyond this gate provides a pleasant riverside excursion, much used by local anglers, but this is the only entrance and exit so, unless you particularly want another short trip down to the River, keep going along the pavement and I promise you a lovely walk along the River edge in just under half a mile.

Avoiding the oak tree growing out of the pavement, keep on, past some poplars and two low aluminium barriers on your right, until you arrive at Clingan Road on the opposite side of the road. Here, you will have reached the high wooden fence which surrounds the Iford Bridge Caravan Park on your right.

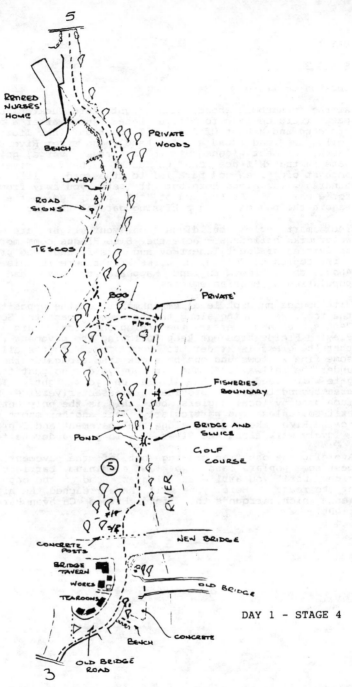

5

RETIRED
NURSES'
HOME

BENCH

PRIVATE
WOODS

LAY-BY

ROAD
SIGNS

TESCOS

BOG

'PRIVATE'

FISHERIES
BOUNDARY

BRIDGE AND
SLUICE

POND

GOLF
COURSE

5

RIVER

CONCRETE
POSTS

NEW BRIDGE

BRIDGE
TAVERN

WORKS

OLD BRIDGE

TEAROOMS

DAY 1 - STAGE 4

BENCH

CONCRETE

OLD BRIDGE
ROAD

3

DAY 1

STAGE 4

Iford to Riverside Avenue

Arriving at a small bed of shrubs and flowers in the pavement,
protected by black and white posts, turn left down into Old
Bridge Road and follow the road past a Tea Room and a grassy
area with benches by the river to the Old Iford Bridge. Four
arches span the River but many more carry the road over once
boggy grassland on the other side. Do not go over the
bridge but, keeping to the old road, pass another area of
grass and more benches to the new Christchurch Road with the
Bridge Tavern on the left corner. Carefully cross the road
and go between low concrete posts on the other side to join a
path across a further grassy area, signposted "Holdenhurst
Village". By the first bench, join a path coming from your
left and follow the riverside path (the one I promised you
earlier) with Iford Golf Course on the opposite bank.

Past a pond on your left and over a sluice gate bridge, keep
straight on, ignoring paths going off to your left. A
boundary sign by the River edge shows how jealously guarded
are the fishing rights along this River. On the upriver
side of the sign, the rights belong to Throop Fisheries whilst
the downriver side belongs to the Christchurch Angling Club -
and never the twain shall meet. Sadly, Throop Fisheries
cause us to lose the River shortly and also prevent us from
joining its banks again until we reach Throop Mill.

Past a solitary willow tree to the left of the path, you
arrive at a stile in the fence straddling the path. Do not
cross over the stile! This is Throop Fisheries land.
Instead, turn sharp left and follow the yellow footpath arrow,
bending around into some trees where you join the path which
goes around and above a bog to come out, past a gate, onto
Riverside Avenue.

Immediately opposite, as you emerge from the trees, is a huge
Tesco superstore so, if you need provisions for the rest of
Day 1 and before you get to Parley or Longham, pop in,
although our creed is to support the little village shops
which we will pass on our way, isn't it?

Having successfully resisted the temptation, turn right and
use the pavement on the Tesco side until it runs out by the
"Dead End", "People Walking" and "Road Narrows" signs. Here,
there is a small lay-by on the left as a steep bank marks the
edge of one of the few remaining fields after the building of
the 1st stage of the Royal Bournemouth Hospital which was
completed in 1991 on what had once been Green Belt land.
Cross back to the RH side of the road and face any oncoming
traffic, with trees on your right and views into the River
valley. At a LH bend in the road, you can see the Hospital

away on your left just before a gated entrance into Private
Woods. Shortly, the old established Retired Nurses National
Home is passed on the left. This was here long before Tesco
or the Hospital and once stood in splendid isolation but the
residents have had to endure colossal building works on their
doorstep for several years - with more to come, I'm afraid.

..down into Old Bridge Road
- Iford - Day 1, Page 21

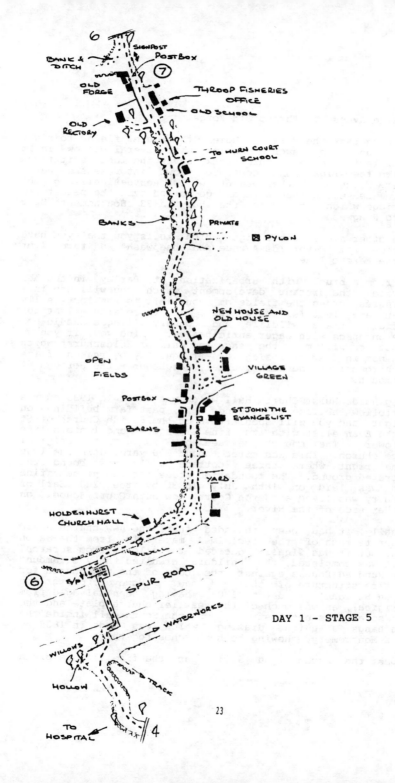

6

BANK & DITCH

SIGNPOST
POSTBOX

⑦

OLD FORGE

THROOP FISHERIES OFFICE

OLD SCHOOL

OLD RECTORY

TO MURN COURT SCHOOL

BANKS

PRIVATE

☒ PYLON

NEW HOUSE AND OLD HOUSE

OPEN FIELDS

VILLAGE GREEN

POSTBOX

ST JOHN THE EVANGELIST

BARNS

YARD.

HOLDENHURST CHURCH HALL

⑥

S/P

SPUR ROAD

WATERWORKS

WILLOWS

HOLLOW

TRACK

TO HOSPITAL

4

DAY 1 - STAGE 5

DAY 1

STAGE 5

Riverside Avenue to Throop Old Forge

Continuing past the Nurses' Home, there are fields to right
and left until you reach a hollow with several willows in it
on your left. Here, a farm track leaves the lane as it turns
round to the right and continues down into Wessex Water
Recovery Works - a rather quaint whilst aesthetically correct
title. Leave the road here and go up and over the pedestrian
footbridge which straddles the busy A338, Bournemouth Spur
Road to Ringwood.

On the other side, pass a sign which tells you that you have
just come from "Riverside Avenue and Sheepwash" and turn right
onto the tarmac lane.

Apart from a brush with urbanization at Parley, in another
five miles, the distant development which you will see in a
few minutes across the fields on your left is the last really
built-up area in this whole trek, so those with a lust for
open fields, trees, wildlife and country villages should now
plunge on apace with eager anticipation. Mind you, if you go
too fast you will miss the peace and calm of Holdenhurst which
now stands in fear of losing its tranquility by reason of its
ever-encroaching, and much younger, neighbour - the Borough of
Bournemouth.

Passing Holdenhurst Church Hall which was built in 1933 on the
left, follow the lane as it bends left, past farm buildings on
the right, and you will soon arrive at the Parish Church of St
John the Evangelist with its fine lychgate and lantern-like
bell tower. The church we see now is not the original
village church. This was sited about 100 yards down the lane
on the right where three cottage walls now bound the
consecrated ground. The foundation stone for the present fine
church was laid on 18th July 1833 by the 2nd Earl of
Malmesbury who lived at Heron Court, now Hurn Court School, on
the other side of the River.

Originally, it had been intended that the new church would
incorporate much of the reclaimed materials from the Saxon
church, but it was finally decided to build it from scratch.
When it was completed, the builders credited the vast amount
of One Hundred Pounds against the cost of the new church for
the entire structure of the old one. However, one of the
bells in St John's is dated 1702, having been salvaged from
the original, as was much of the earlier church plate and the
font - so all was not lost. On the South wall inside the
church hangs a unique drawing, which was made in 1839 by
Cecilia Montgomery, showing both churches together.

Just past the church, you arrive at the fine village green

which, by its very presence, confirms the antiquity of Holdenhurst. Marauding cars are prevented from spoiling the green by an encircling row of low timber posts and, for our convenience, a bench has been provided under the trees at this end - also a post box and a telephone box.

At the opposite end of the green are two particularly fine brick houses. The larger LH building is the "New House" which was built in the 18th Century by William Clapcott, whilst the thatched RH building is the very much older "Old House" - quite logical, really. The deeds relating to the "Old House" describe it as the former Hospice of St Mary Magdalene and this house is thought to be the oldest in Holdenhurst

Passing along the road, there are now open fields on the left, mostly atop a grassy embankment along the rest of the road, whilst the views into the fields on the right are frequently blocked by a ribbon of woods alongside the road. An unusual feature of this stretch of road is the array of still working gas lamps - but for how long?, I wonder.

Shortly, a row of iron railings on the right indicates the boundary of Hurn Court School and the Malmesbury Estate, all of which is private and keeps us away from the Stour, for a while at least. Keep on, past the ribbon of woods, past the turning into the School and on, past the Old Village School, Throop Fisheries Ticket Office and some cottages on the right. If you would like to visit the closed Throop Mill, about 800 yards further down the road (and which you have to go past, anyway) pop into the Ticket Office and ask if Ron Biles, the Water Bailiff, and son of the last miller at Throop Mill, has the time to show you around and, at the same time, to dispense some of his vast knowledge of the Mill and the surrounding area of Throop which he clearly loves. A short detail of Mr Biles' story is included in Stage 6 notes.

Opposite the Old School stands the Old Rectory which was built in 1833 by the Rev Hopkins, the incumbent of St John's at the time, for Rev Biver, his assistant parish priest.

Adjacent to the Rectory's boundary wall stands the Old Forge. beyond which, after a post box, a lane turns off left whilst the signpost confirms that you are, indeed, still heading for Throop.

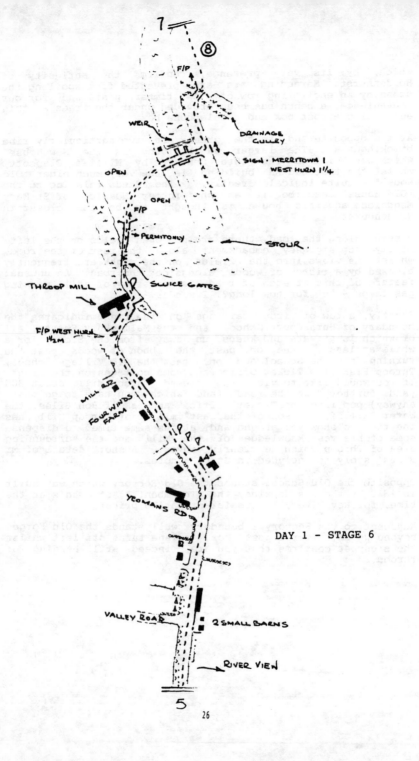

7

⑧

F/P

WEIR

DRAINAGE GULLEY

SIGN · MERRITOWN 1
WEST HURN 1¼

OPEN

OPEN

F/P

PERMIT ONLY

STOUR.

THROOP MILL

SLUICE GATES

F/P WEST HURN
1½ M

MILL RD

FOUR WINDS FARM

YEOMANS RD

DAY 1 - STAGE 6

VALLEY ROAD

2 SMALL BARNS

RIVER VIEW

5

DAY 1

STAGE 6

Throop Old Forge to Throop Weir

With glimpses of our River down on your right and with the
occasional barn and house to left and right, keep straight on
past Valley Road, Yeomans Road and Mill Road on your left.
Shortly after Four Winds Farm on the left, you arrive at the
huge bulk of Throop Mill where a Footpath signpost on the
right proclaims "Public Footpath West Hurn 1.1/2 miles".

For a short history of the Mill, have a look at the notice
board which Ron Biles unveiled in the Car Park in 1986. On a
more personal level, Ron's father, Cis Biles, was the last
working miller at Throop Mill, having started here in 1929 for
Parsons and Sons. When the Mill was taken over in 1957 by
Heygates of Northampton, Cis continued working as a miller and
stayed on when it was converted into a warehouse in 1972. The
Mill was truly Cis Biles' life for, at the age of 82, whilst
painting a small window frame high up on the outside of the
Mill, he tragically collapsed and died, falling to the ground,
on May 20th 1981.

Follow the path between the back of the Mill and the railings
and go round to where the path turns left and follows the edge
of the River to the concrete path over the sluice gates. It
is only in the recent past that the route of the River, which
used to follow this top level and was the cause of much annual
flooding, was diverted to the route which you can see over to
your right and which you will soon cross by a new footbridge.
In the River below the sluice gates, I was particularly lucky
to see a fine Great Crested Grebe who, Mr Biles informed me,
is the best fisherman in the whole area.

Anyway, keep to the path as it turns across the open grassy
area with River on either side and, passing the "Fishing
Permit Holders Only" path, go straight on to cross the Stour
on the modern steel bridge with all sorts of level controls
and a weir which causes wild turbulence under the bridge. On
the other side, turn left at the Footpath sign "Merritown 1"
and, keeping to the wire fence, cross the small bridge over a
drainage gulley to the stile ahead of you.

This is highly significant step which you are about to take as
this is the first stile on the Stour Valley Path. So start
practicing your stile-climbing technique now, then follow the
Footpath sign along the side of the River.

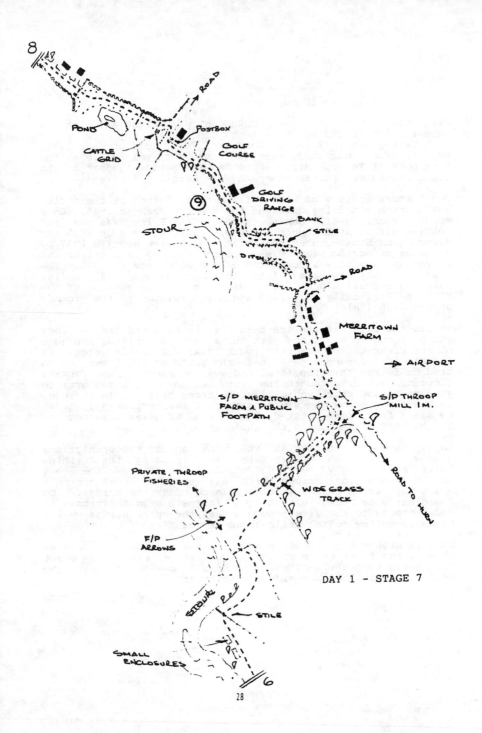

8

POND

CATTLE
GRID

ROAD

POSTBOX

GOLF
COURSE

9

GOLF
DRIVING
RANGE

BANK

STOUR

STILE

DITCH

ROAD

MERRITOWN
FARM

AIRPORT

S/D MERRITOWN
FARM & PUBLIC
FOOTPATH

S/D THROOP
MILL 1M.

PRIVATE. THROOP
FISHERIES

WIDE GRASS
TRACK

ROAD TO HURN

F/P
ARROWS

DAY 1 - STAGE 7

STOUR

STILE

SMALL
ENCLOSURES

6

28

DAY 1

STAGE 7

Throop Weir to Parley Court Pond

Not too close to the River, keep to the RH side of two small
wooded areas enclosed by low wire fences and head for the
stile in the end of the field fence where it meets the River
edge. Over the stile, follow the River more closely now,
with a few bushes right in the water when it is running full.
If you are wondering what the prevalent noise is, it's the
Hurn (Bournemouth) Airport just beyond the fields to the North
of Merritown Farm. Anyway, over the next stile by the River
edge, turn right and head across the field to the next stile
in the far LH corner. The true path actually goes straight
on here, not diagonally, but it turns at right angles when it
gets to the footpath arrow in the corner by the "Private
Throop Fisheries" sign. So, diagonally, we arrive at the
next stile and, over it, find ourselves in a very wide grassy
track between parallel hedges. The track is reduced to more
conventional width by encroaching bushes and brambles. Keep
on the track as it loses its grassy covering and becomes less
pleasant in the last part where the mud is kept from drying by
the shade from the trees on the left.

Emerging now, over a stile onto a junction of a farm track
left and a tarmac lane right and with a steep bank facing you,
turn left and go past the sign for "Merritown Farm and Public
Footpath Only". Through the farm buildings, take special
note of the farmhouse. Unfortunately, this is the rear of
the building but the front which faces the Airport has a
particularly fine Georgian style facade with a huge stone
staircase and pillars either side of the main door. This
building is the central section of a formerly grand house
which had vast wings at either end and, internally, the
farmhouse still retains some superb Georgian panelling.

Keep straight on through the farmyard and, as the track turns
right, go over a stile by the farm gate facing you and keep
close to the banked hedge on the RH side of the field beyond
the stile until you reach another stile at the end of this
hedge.

Over this stile, the path turns sharp left onto a grassy
stretch between the high fence of the Golf Driving Range on
your right and a bank down into the field you have just left
on your left. Follow the guard bank and the fence and keep
on round to the right as you briefly come to the edge of the
Stour again. Past the office and buildings of the Range and
Golf Course, join a tarmac drive which ends at a junction of
farm tracks as the drive turns away to the right. At the
postbox on the RH corner, turn right and instantly left again,
signposted "Parley Court Farm".

After two gates across the track, you pass a duckpond on your left which has a resident gaggle of geese together with the usual duck fraternity.

Past the pond and a farm track coming in from your left, go through the gate by a cattle grid and keep on the wide gravel drive past a couple of houses on your right.

..the central section of a formerly grand house
- Merritown Farm, Hurn Airport - Day 1, Page 29

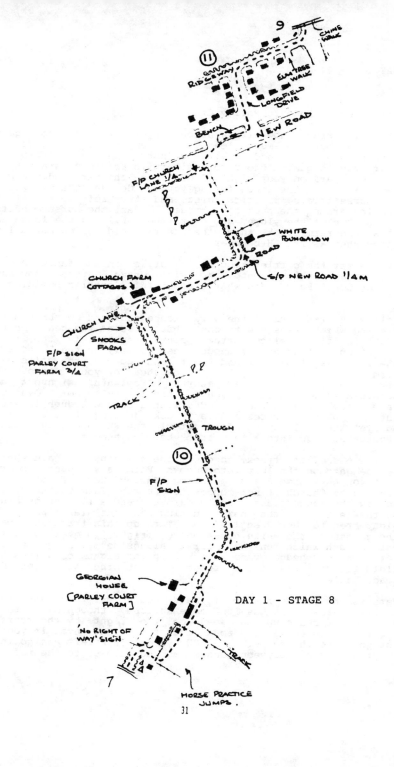

9

CHINE WALK

11

RIDGEWAY

ELM TREE WALK

LONGFIELD DRIVE

NEW ROAD

BENCH

F/P CHURCH LANE 1/4

WHITE BUNGALOW

ROAD

CHURCH FARM COTTAGES

S/P NEW ROAD '11 AM

CHURCH LANE

SNOOKS FARM

F/P SIGN
PARLEY COURT FARM 3/4

P. P

TRACK

TROUGH

10

F/P SIGN

GEORGIAN HOUSE
[PARLEY COURT FARM]

DAY 1 - STAGE 8

'NO RIGHT OF WAY' SIGN

TRACK

7

HORSE PRACTICE JUMPS.

31

DAY 1

STAGE 8

Parley Court Pond to Parley Cross

This wide track, now with a ditch on either side, looks quite inviting but we must leave it temporarily because the farmstead which straddles it is not keen on visitors. A perfectly adequate detour for walkers is provided, starting in the next yard on your right. Go into the yard and you will see a stile in the fence facing you. Go over the stile into the horse trials practice area and turn left up the slight incline around the back of a house. Past the horses shelter at the top of the slope, go over the stile in the fence and cross the farm track into the next field which has a long brick shed as its LH boundary.

Just after the cattle trough, a stile in the fence on your left takes you back onto the wide gravel drive, now past Parley Court Farm - and what a beautiful Georgian building it is.

Follow the track until the wire fence ends and go through the opening which takes you to the other side of the hedge on the right (a faint yellow arrow points vaguely in the right direction). Behind the hedge, keep closely to the LH edge of the field as it bends round left and go over the stile by a farm gate with another yellow arrow ahead of you. Across the next long field, you pass another "Footpath" signpost just before a farm gate facing you in the far LH corner. Over the gate, keep close to the RH hedge with a cattle trough inserted into it, past two gates and a track joining from the left. Go over the stile by the farm gate in the RH corner by another "Footpath" sign into a farm track between hedges.

At the end of the track, go over the stile by the gate where, by the gate on the left into Snooks Farm, a signpost confirms that you have come 3/4 mile from "Parley Court Farm". Turn right onto Church Lane, opposite Church Farm Cottages, and follow the hedged lane, past a farmyard and a fine brick house on the left, to the next turning on the left which is signposted to "New Road 1/4". Turn up this track and, past the garden of the white house on your right, go over the stile onto a path which runs at first alongside a hedge on your left. As the hedge runs out, keep straight on across the field to the stile in the fence on the other side, into New Road, Parley.

Here is the urbanization I said would be the last truly built-up area. It has its compensations, though. There is a parade of shops up the road on the right, by the traffic lights. Cross over the road and turn right, even if you're not going to the shops. In 100 yards, turn left and go into Longfield Drive, between houses and bungalows, to the far end where a track crosses from left to right. Turn right and, with a hedged field to your left, keep straight on, past houses to right and left, to the road ahead. Turn left here past another bench on the near LH corner and a bus stop for a Wilts and Dorset 134 in the main road. This would take you directly to Longham but don't be tempted. The next part of the walk takes you along the very edge of the River Stour through some particularly pleasant pasture.

..the last truly built-up area
- Parley Cross - Day 1, Page 32

33

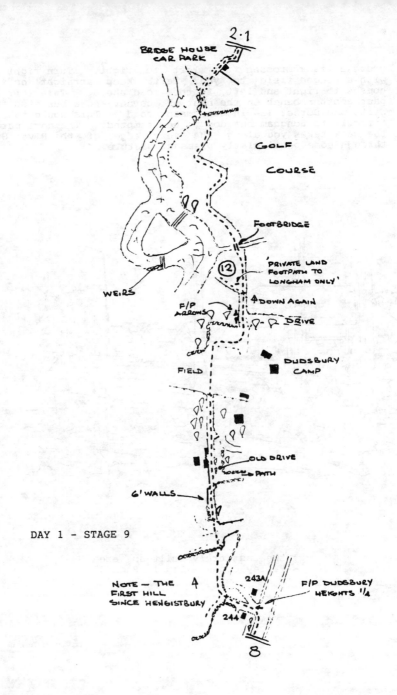

2·1

BRIDGE HOUSE
CAR PARK

GOLF

COURSE

FOOTBRIDGE

WEIRS

12

'PRIVATE LAND
FOOTPATH TO
LONGHAM ONLY'

↓ DOWN AGAIN

F/P
↗↗↗

↘ DRIVE

DUDSBURY
CAMP

FIELD

OLD DRIVE

PATH

6' WALLS

DAY 1 - STAGE 9

NOTE — THE   4
FIRST HILL
SINCE HENGISTBURY

243A

244

F/P DUDSBURY
HEIGHTS ¼

8

34

DAY 1

STAGE 9

Parley Cross to Longham

Just 100 yards up the hill, turn left into a track which
instantly splits into two - the right fork being to a private
house whilst the left fork has a signpost "Footpath Dudsbury
Heights 1/4". This track narrows to a path at No 244, after
which you go over a stile into the field where the path is
joined by another from down hill on your left. Here, the
signpost includes our first Day's target - "Longham 1.1/4",
most of which is along the edge of the Stour.

Turn sharp right and go up the hill (the first incline since
we left Hengistbury Head, 9 miles ago). That is why I have
included some hilly diversions when we are clear of these
urban areas. At the top of the hill, go through the kissing
gate at the end of the hedge into the driveway to River Park
Inn. Keep straight on across the drive and over a stile onto
the narrow pathway opposite, between a hedge on the left and a
field boundary of thin trees on your right. Now following
the 6ft high brick wall of a house on your left, a grassy path
shoots off at right angles on your right. Keep straight on,
between a LH wooden fence and a RH wire fence with a lovely
Victorian house and fine gardens lurking in the woods behind
it. Mind the tree roots in the path here - we don't want you
breaking a leg before you reach the pastoral splendours to
come.

A few yards further on, go over the stile into the field
beyond. The buildings in this field, on your right as you
cross over, belong to the Girl Guides so I wish you luck as
you gingerly cross to the other side - you are at great risk
from marauding females. Now, safely arriving at the car
parking area, turn right and leave by the field entrance down
onto a driveway. Immediately turn off the drive by going
left, down a narrow, fenced pathway which is indicated by
yellow footpath arrows. So our hill climbing exercise for the
day is already over. You are now descending from Dudsbury
Camp, the Iron Age hill fort, barely recognizable as such with
houses surrounding it but the Girl Guides have taken over its
defence quite admirably.

As you drop down on this other side towards the River, a look
back will show that Dudsbury is on quite a significant ridge
above the Stour and would have been reasonably defendable -
but not from the other three sides. Over the stile at the
end of the fenced path, a sign reminds us that this is "Private
Land. Footpath to Longham Only" and, descending the hill
between gorse bushes and the Dudsbury Golf Course, the view of
the River as it meanders across the fertile plain is quite
beautiful. At the bottom of the hill, go over the footbridge
which crosses a stream as it emerges from the Golf Course and

runs into the River. Here, the River has divided itself - undecided which way it preferred to wander - and both branches have pleasant weirs to break the smooth flow which otherwise typifies this stretch of the Stour.

Keeping near to the boundary fence, follow the River for 1/2 mile until the fence almost meets the River edge. Here, go over the stile onto a very narrow stretch right on the River bank. Mind that you don't fall in before, sadly, the path turns away from the River in a few yards. Now, with the car park of the Bridge Hotel on the left and a mowed field on the right, the path becomes contained between chain link fences to Longham.

No end of buses go through Longham (consult your Wilts and Dorset timetable), on the left to Bournemouth and Poole and on the right to Ferndown, so there is no shortage of accommodation - and Longham has Inns and bed and breakfasts itself.

No end of buses go through
Longham - Day 1, This Page

Thanks to Wilts and Dorset for
letting me use their 'Busabout'
logo.

..complete with its
own resident Saint
- Ashington Lane -
Day 2, Page 53

..observe the River
level gauges -
Charlton Marshall
- Day 2, Page 66

DAY 2 - INTRODUCTION

Longham to Crawford Bridge

A short stroll across fields takes us to the tiny village of Hampreston from where much varied farmland takes us to historic Canford School by the edge of the Stour. From here, a carriage drive and country lanes lead to the footpath to Eye Bridge, next to the old Roman ford between Badbury Rings and Hamworthy Quay.

Through the National Trust's huge estate of Kingston Lacy, the route goes on to the Saxon village of Shapwick and thence across riverside fields to the Day's end at Crawford Bridge in the lee of Spetisbury village. This is a fine, level walk in tranquil farmland for most of the Day where birds and cattle reign supreme and where provisions can be obtained from a couple of cosy Inns on the way.

	STAGE	MILES	TOTAL
1	Longham to Hampreston	1.25	1.25
2	Hampreston to Stapehill Road	.75	2
3	Stapehill Road to Canford Bottom	.75	2.75
4	Canford Bottom to Canford Riverside	.50	3.25
5	Canford Riverside to Merley Bridge	1.50	4.75
6	Merley Bridge to Ashington Lane	1.25	6
7	Ashington Lane to Eye Bridge	1	7
8	Eye Bridge to Cowgrove	1	8
9	Cowgrove to New Barn Farm	1.50	9.50
10	New Barn Farm to Shapwick	2	11.50
11	Shapwick to Crawford Bridge	1	12.50

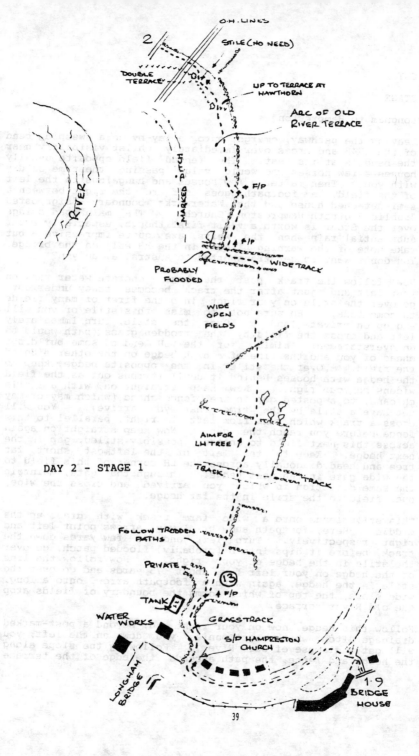

O.H. LINES

STILE (NO NEED)

2

DOUBLE TERRACE

UP TO TERRACE AT HAWTHORN

ARC OF OLD RIVER TERRACE

RIVER

MARKED DITCH

F/P

F/P

WIDE TRACK

PROBABLY FLOODED

WIDE OPEN FIELDS

AIM FOR LH TREE

TRACK

TRACK

DAY 2 - STAGE 1

FOLLOW TRODDEN PATHS

PRIVATE

13

F/P

TANK

GRASSTRACK

WATER WORKS

S/D HAMPRESTON CHURCH

LONGHAM BRIDGE

1·9

BRIDGE HOUSE

DAY 2

STAGE 1

Longham to Hampreston

Leaving the pathway, emerge onto a lay-by on a sweeping bend of the A348 and cross over immediately whilst visibility near the bend is at its best. The fenced field opposite usually houses a few horses who would value passing the time of day with you. Then ,after a few houses and bungalows to the left of the field, a footpath goes off to the right between a semi-detached house and the Waterworks boundary - signposted "Public Footpath Hampreston Church". The main road bridge over the Stour is worth a visit first though, especially after substantial rain when the weirs are quite impressive - but take note of the warning plaque in the RH wall on the bridge. You don't want to get transported to Australia, do you?

Now, follow the track past the huge concrete water tank on your left and, just after the track becomes grassy underfoot, go over the stile on your right into the first of many fields to come today. Be sure not to miss this stile or you will end up on private land. Over the stile, turn immediately left and cross the field by the trodden grass (path would be an overstatement), aiming for the LH end of some buildings ahead of you and the line of a high hedge on the other side of the field. Over the stile in the opposite hedge, keep to the hedge with houses behind it until it runs out as the field widens on your right. Now keep straight on, with a little chicane, to a posted gap in the fence ahead (which may or may not have a stile by the time that you arrive). You will cross a track which runs from left to right, parallel to this fence before you reach the gap. Now keep straight on again across this next field to another, possibly stiled, gap in the next hedge. Keep to the left of the leftmost, short, fat tree and head diagonally across the LH corner of this field to the wide gate in the next hedge. Through that gate, maintain the same direction in which you arrived and cross the wide, open field to the stile in the far hedge.

This stile leads onto a wide farm track with grass up the middle. Here, footpath and bridleway arrows point left and right respectively. Turn left and, a few yards down the track, before it dips into a (probably) flooded patch, go over the stile in the hedge on your right. Now follow the line of the hedge on your left for about 75 yards and go over the stile in the hedge, again with a footpath arrow, onto a long, wide slope, the top of which forms the boundary of fields atop the old River terrace.

Follow this hedge, now on your right and, beyond a post-marked drainage ditch which accompanies you down on the left, you will get a glimpse of our River. Following the slope along the hedge and fence, the path ascends the edge of the terrace

by a hawthorn bush and now follows the top of the terrace.
This terrace path takes an arc of almost a quarter of a circle
along our route and is soon enhanced by a stile to nowhere. It
stands astride our path in a short segment of fence which
branches out from the right near another hawthorn bush -
but you can walk around it if you need to save your energy for
all the stiles to come. Here, the steep terrace divides into
two shallower terraces just before we pass under high overhead
elecricity cables.

..rebuilt..between 1896 and 1897 in
the Decorative style - All Saints
Church, Hampreston - Day 2, Page 43

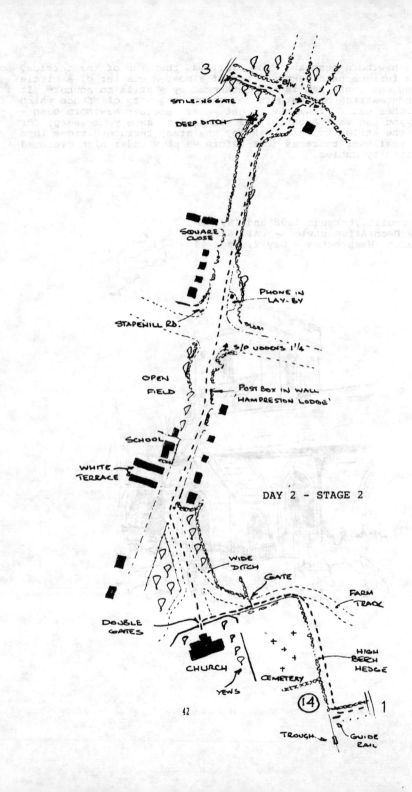

DAY 2 - STAGE 2

DAY 2

STAGE 2

Hampreston to Stapehill Road

At the end of the terrace path, with a wire fence facing you,
turn right over the stile and follow the line of the hedge on
your left in the next field. Within a few yards, the hedge
becomes a high beech hedge with Hampreston cemetery behind it.
Follow the footpath alongside this hedge to its end where it
turns left onto a farm track. Keep to the hedge and the new
hedge and wire fence until you reach the old brick wall which
surrounds the original churchyard and cemetery. A few yards
along this wall, you come to the double wooden gated entrance
to All Saints Church, Hampreston.

This church was largely rebuilt by Romaine, Walker and Tanner
between 1896 and 1897 in the Decorative style although a
church has stood on this site for centuries. Hamme Prestone
was Ham Chamberlayne until 1293, probably after Aiulfus the
Chamberlain who possessed it until the time of William the
Conqueror.

Leave the churchyard by this gate which led to the church door
onto the long and wide driveway. This runs between a wide,
tree-filled ditch on the right and a wide grass verge on the
left. At the end of the drive, it opens onto a tarmac road
by a footpath arrow and a sign "To the Church". Bear right
here and cross to the pavement on the other side of the road.
This runs past the Village School on the left and continues,
past a postbox in the wall of Hampreston Lodge on the RH side
of the road. At the crossroads ahead, with fields on three
of the corners and a house on the fourth, a sign points toward
"Uddens 1/4" whilst a visitor sign points to "Knoll Gardens".
Cross the road, taking care as it is very busy at times, into
Stapehill Road opposite. Keep to the RH side of the road,
passing a lay-by and a telephone box on your right.

After a row of houses and Square Close on your left, the road
bends in about 200 yards where, on the right, a footpath goes
off into a field just after a red-brick house.

Cross over to the LH side and, at a bridleway sign, turn left
onto a track which runs between hedges with a ditch on either
side.

On the way along this track, you pass another defunct stile
across your way. No gate, no fence, just a stile - so keep
straight on.

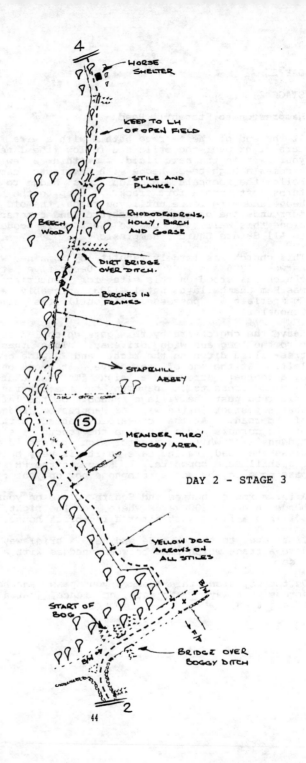

4

HORSE SHELTER

KEEP TO LH OF OPEN FIELD

STILE AND PLANKS.

RHODODENDRONS, HOLLY, BIRCH AND GORSE

BEECH WOOD

DIRT BRIDGE OVER DITCH.

BIRCHES IN FRAMES

STAPENHILL ABBEY

(15)

MEANDER THRO' BOGGY AREA.

DAY 2 - STAGE 3

YELLOW DCC ARROWS ON ALL STILES

START OF BOG

BRIDGE OVER BOGGY DITCH

BM

2

DAY 2

STAGE 3

Stapehill Road to Canford Bottom

You are now in the realms of "primeval" bogs, so tread warily.
Really, the track is fine but the sudden preponderance of
ditches is an initial indication of the wetlands ahead. Follow
the track, now grassy up the middle, to the junction of tracks
ahead where you turn right onto the signed bridleway, with
woods on your left and a fenced field on your right. Here,
the track is wider with ditches on both sides and soon, on the
left, the ditch becomes wider and deeper with several deep,
full drainage ditches running into it from out of the woods.
In about 100 yards, you arrive at a stile ahead of you, a
stile and gate on your right and a stile on your left - all at
once. Climb over the stile on your LEFT into a grassy field
and follow the line of the fenced wood on your left. Head
for a stile in the LH corner of your field and climb over it,
noticing the yellow arrow and DCC Bridleway stamped into it -
as have most of the stiles for the next mile.

Cross the next field, still keeping to the left, and climb
over the stile in the fence into a really boggy wood with
ditches and deep, still water bordering the path. Meander
through this wood (on the path, of course) and, with great
relief, cross the stile after a RH bend in the path back into
open fields. At this stile you have a good view of Stapehill
Abbey across the field ahead of you. Turn instantly left
after the stile and follow the LH edge of the field, still
with a drainage ditch on your left. Over another stile into
another open field with new birch trees enclosed by protective
frames, keep straight on and over yet another stile, a dirt
bridge over a ditch and on, through a thicket of
rhododendrons, holly, birch and gorse for (count with head
down to avoid overhanging branches) 175 yards. Then cross
over a stile between two short steel fence sections and out,
over a plank bridge, into another open field. Keep to the
left edge, now with more open views into the neighbouring open
field, and go over the ditch ahead of you by using the broken
planks. Now you are in a field with hawthorn bushes, still
with the ditch on your left, probably inhabited by a couple of
inquisitive ponies who share a convenienet shelter, behind
which our path passes.

In this field, a fine green woodpecker was busily helping
himself to some tasty morsels when I arrived but, needless to
say, he didn't stay long after I had plunged headlong out of
the thicket.

After the relatively restful progress which was possible on
Day 1, isn't it nice to have so many stiles to exercise your
legs over today? There are lots more to come.

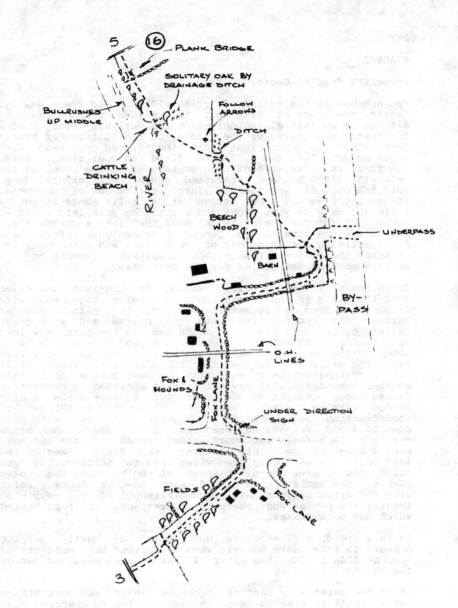

5　⑯　— PLANK BRIDGE

SOLITARY OAK BY
DRAINAGE DITCH

BULLRUSHES
UP MIDDLE

FOLLOW
ARROWS

DITCH

CATTLE
DRINKING
BEACH

RIVER

BEECH
WOOD

UNDERPASS

BARN

BY-
PASS

O.H.
LINES

FOX &
HOUNDS

FOX LANE

UNDER DIRECTION
SIGN

FIELDS

FOX LANE

3

DAY 2 - STAGE 4

DAY 2

STAGE 4

Canford Bottom to Canford Riverside

Leave the horses' field by the stile set in the fence at the
end of their field and follow the grassy track, with ditches
left and right, until it emerges into Fox Lane. Turn sharp
left and cut across the grass verge near the LH hedge and -
very carefully - cross the road to the opposite verge. Walk
underneath the direction sign and turn right into Fox Lane Mk
II which was all part of the same lane until the road was
realigned during construction of the Wimborne By-Pass - and
the Fox and Hounds was by-passed at the same time.

Follow the hedged lane, past the Fox and Hounds entrance - or
via the Fox and Hounds if necessary - and, when the lane turns
left, go right into the cul-de-sac, taking note of the fine
red-brick house ahead of you before you turn.

Go under the overhead electric cables and then through the
double gates which straddle the lane. Follow the hedge around
to the left and, instead of continuing under the By-Pass
underpass, keep going left and cross over the stile at the
side of a farm gate.

Ahead of you is a wood and there is a barn over the fence on
your left, However, at the stile, aim for a farm gate which
you will see at the RH end of the wood, passing once more
unedrneath the O/H cables. On arrival at the gate, you will
see a stile alongside it. Go over the stile and maintain your
original direction towards another gate and stile which lead
you onto a bridge across a drainage ditch. Over this next
stile, follow the direction of the Footpath arrow and aim to
the left of a solitary oak. You will be walking diagonally
away from the wire fence that you have just crossed and
getting nearer to the River which flows from right to left as
you approach it. Past the oak, a single hawthorn bush marks
the spot where you cross another drainage gulley near to where
the embankment is suitably low for the cattle to have a good
drink from the River - and a bathe from the beach.

All along this bank of the River, there are beeches and rushes
and the path is very clear and pleasant. This is the start
of a fine stretch which will be of particular interest to bird
watchers and is in marked contrast to the primeval bog section
which you endured on the other side of Fox Lane.

Now cross over a stile in a gulley and a plank bridge with no
hand rails into the next field.

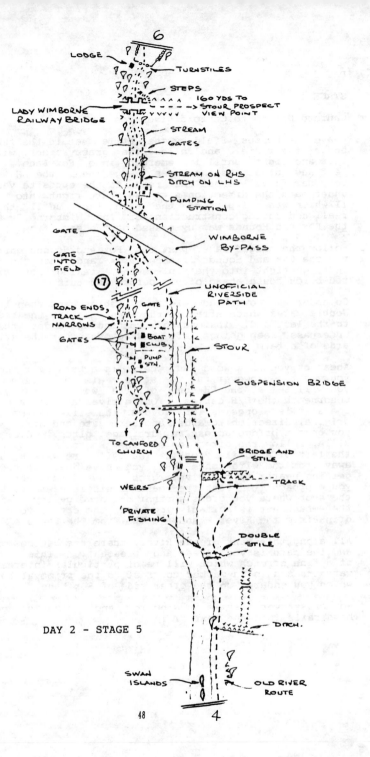

6

LODGE

TURNSTILES

STEPS

160 YDS TO
STOUR PROSPECT
VIEW POINT

LADY WIMBORNE
RAILWAY BRIDGE

STREAM

GATES

STREAM ON RHS
DITCH ON LHS

PUMPING
STATION

GATE

WIMBORNE
BY-PASS

GATE
INTO
FIELD

(17)

UNOFFICIAL
RIVERSIDE
PATH

ROAD ENDS,
TRACK
NARROWS

GATE

GATES

BOAT
CLUB

STOUR

PUMP
STN.

SUSPENSION BRIDGE

TO CANFORD
CHURCH

BRIDGE AND
STILE

TRACK

WEIRS

'PRIVATE
FISHING'

DOUBLE
STILE

DAY 2 - STAGE 5

DITCH.

SWAN
ISLANDS

OLD RIVER
ROUTE

48

4

DAY 2

STAGE 5

Canford Riverside to Merley Bridge

Keep on along the River edge and note the terracing of the old
River's route close by on your right.   Here is a regular
nesting place for swans on the little islands in the River and
here is where I caught the sudden brilliant flash of a
kingfisher which I had disturbed.

At a tree by the next drainage ditch is the next stile which
you cross into another field.   Over the River, many of
Canford School's buildings come into view, some functional,
some fine and some historic.

The grant of Canford manor was given to Walter de Eureux, 2nd
Earl of Salisbury who died in 1196, although the manor itself
had existed long before the arrival of William the Conqueror.
Walter's successor, William Longespee (or Longsword) laid one
of the foundation stones of Salisbury Cathedral in 1220 at the
same time as he began to rebuild the Manor House here at
Canford.   The oldest remaining part of the present house is
John of Gaunt's kitchen which is visible from the footpath on
our side of the River.   This dates back to the 14th and 15th
Centuries.

From our vantage point, the most visible parts of greatest
interest are Nineveh Court on the LH end of John of Gaunt's
kitchen and the arched Victoria Tower at the other end.
Nineveh Court was built in 1851 specifically to house the many
artifacts brought back for Sir John Guest, the owner at the
time, from Sir Austin Layard's excavation of the ancient
Assyrian capital.   Sadly, although Layard later received an
Honorary Degree from Oxford University and the Freedom of
London for his discovery and excavation of the "majestic
capital of Assyria", it was later shown that he had, in fact,
excavated the city of Calah, about 20 miles away from Nineveh.
Similarly, in death, confusion over Layard's whereabouts
seemed just as deep.   Just before the path at the South-West
corner of Canford Church stands the red granite slab of
Layard's tomb on which we are informed that he was, indeed,
the "Discoverer of Nineveh".   In fact, following his later
career in the world of politics, he was cremated in Woking in
1894 and his ashes were buried there, not at Canford at all.
More conventionally now, to the Victoria Tower.   This was
added to the house at the time of its greatest rebuild in 1848
by Sir John Barry, still for Sir John Guest, and is noticeably
in the stile of Barry's most famous building - the Houses of
Parliament.

Now follow the River to a double stile next to the notice
"Private Fishing - Wimborne and District Angling Club".   I

wonder if the kingfisher or the two cormorants which were cruising the river had seen this sign.

In the next field, the path veers slightly away from the River and, about 250 yards from the last stile, you climb over the stile in the wire fence directly onto a farm track where you turn instantly left and then right. Cross over the bridge over a ditch and, by another gate across your path, climb over the stile into another wide field (the last) with weirs across the River to your left. Head across this field for another 250 yards to the fine suspension bridge across the river. Stop to admire the view from the bridge, and the slender bridge itself, and notice how smoothly the River flows at this point, perfect for the School's boating club. Also notice the many coots and moorhens who share this part of the River with the School.

Across the River, take the path to the RH side of the tree or to the left if you wish to visit the Parish Church of Canford Magna. This is a very complicated building, never having been demolished and not having endured a major rebuild or Victorian restoration. Saxon in origin, the bulk of the existing church is Norman, dating back to 1120 - 1160, whilst the oldest identifiable section is the chancel of about 1050. The architectural changes evident in the church have been of great assistance to scholars of church architecture in dating other English churches. A rarity amongst English Parish churches, Canford Church is not dedicated to any particular Saint.

Joining the wide drive, known locally as Lady Wimborne's Drive as it was formerly the carriage drive from Wimborne Minster to Canford Manor, continue your journey away from the School and the Church along the shady avenue with firm tarmac under your feet until you have passed the pumping station and the boat houses on your right. Here, as the tarmac gives way to gravel and the track narrows, a gate on your right leads into a field between our path and the river. This is not signposted for public use but is in constant use by the locals for strolling and walking the dog so, if you walk circumspectly and unobtrusively (as I know you always do), a short detour to the River edge would surely offend nobody. However, if you prefer to keep to the straight and narrow - albeit still about 8ft wide - keep straight on for about 1/2 mile until you reach the Wimborne By-Pass as it goes overhead, just where the riverside path comes back from a gate on your right.

After the underpass, and gates to left and right, and after the pumping station on your right, the track becomes elevated with a stream amongst the trees on your right and a deep ditch similarly on your left. Shortly, a strange, immense structure appears incongruously ahead. Such an ornate stone, buttressed, pinnacled and shield-adorned facade as would grace any Gothic edifice (or any Victorian melodrama) that it takes

you completely by surprise. This is the bridge which was
built by Lady Wimborne to carry the railway across her
driveway - the railway being an unwelcome interference which
was, however, integrated into her Ladyship's vista with great
aplomb. If the bridge had to intrude, then let it intrude
magnificently.

Beyond this bridge, which you must treat with the reverence it
deserves, a set of steps has been built into the embankment to
enable a short, ultimately disappointing, detour to be taken
to "Stour Prospect View Point". All the way along the 160
yards path to the viewpoint where the railway bridge across
the River was removed, the view is blocked by trees and shrubs
on either side but, at the end, you do get a glimpse of the
Poole Road bridge to your left where the River runs under the
road leaving Wimborne Minster.

Returning to Lady Wimborne's bridge, continue along the track
to the stone gatehouse and leave through the turnstiles which
stand on either side of a pair of fine, cast-iron and very
ornate gates which are supported on heavy, square stone
columns. Note the sign - "No Cycling, Please".

..then let it intrude
magnificently - Canford
- Day 2, This Page

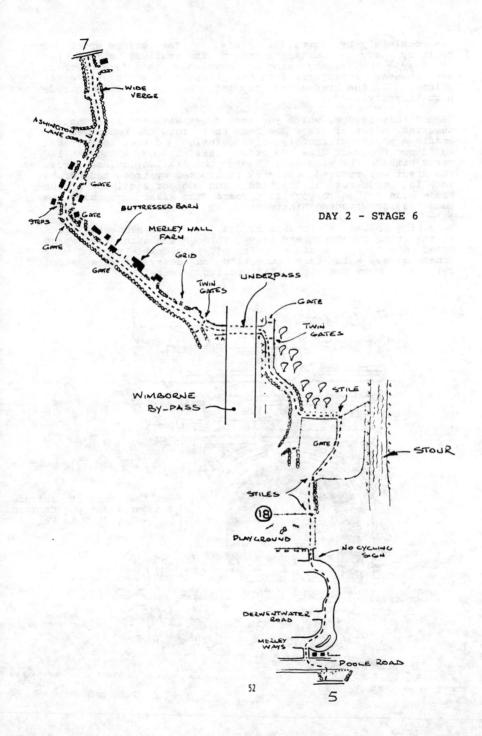

7

WIDE VERGE

ASHINGTON LANE

GATE

STEPS

BUTTRESSED BARN

GATE

MERLEY HALL FARM

GATE

GRID

GATE

TWIN GATES

UNDERPASS

GATE

TWIN GATES

DAY 2 - STAGE 6

WIMBORNE BY-PASS

STILE

STOUR

GATE

STILES

18

PLAYGROUND

NO CYCLING SIGN

DERWENTWATER ROAD

MELLEY WAYS

POOLE ROAD

52

5

DAY 2

STAGE 6

Merley Bridge to Ashington Lane

Carefully cross the busy A349 and, two houses up on the left, take the footpath between the rows of houses away from the main road. Emerging onto an estate of mainly different houses in Merley Ways, keep generally in the same direction and, past Derwentwater Road on your left, take the next footpath between houses nearly opposite you - signed "No Cycling" - and emerge into a smart grassy playground - a small, beautifully neat area and a good retreat for kids and mums alike.

Straight on through the park, go over the stile opposite and follow the fence on your right to another stile. Go over this stile into a field between you and the River, but keep close to this fence which will take you to a final stile leading out of this field onto a narrow path between a fence and a wood . Turn left over the stile onto the path and join the old road, now bisected by the Wimborne By-Pass, here turning right to follow the wood on your right and a hedge on your left behind which thunders the By-Pass traffic.

Go down the slope by the embankment and, through the gate with the blue bridleway arrow and the stricture to "Leave the gate as you found it", go left and underneath the By-Pass. Emerging on the other side, go up the slope and through the gate at the top, back onto the old lane where a new turning space for cars marks the dead-end of what was once a busy linking road.

Past a cattle grid, a gate and a greenhouse on your right, Merley Hall Farmhouse is of special interest. Between the twin gable ends of the two main parts of the house which abut onto the road resides, in much splendour, a Dutch-style gable end complete with its own resident Saint in his niche and a marvellous, studded, wide and wonderful entrance door.

This is Willett Road but, having emerged onto it at the dead-end, there is no indication of its name until you leave it later. However, after this fine house with its flower-bedecked yard and front garden, there is an unusual red-brick buttressed barn, again right on the side of the road, and more individual cottages strung out along the RHS of the road. After a bend in the lane, and past several gates and houses to left and right, pass Ashington Lane on your left and, after two more gates on the left and a short section of wide verge on the right, a derelict stone-mullioned cottage is hidden away behind a hedge on your right.

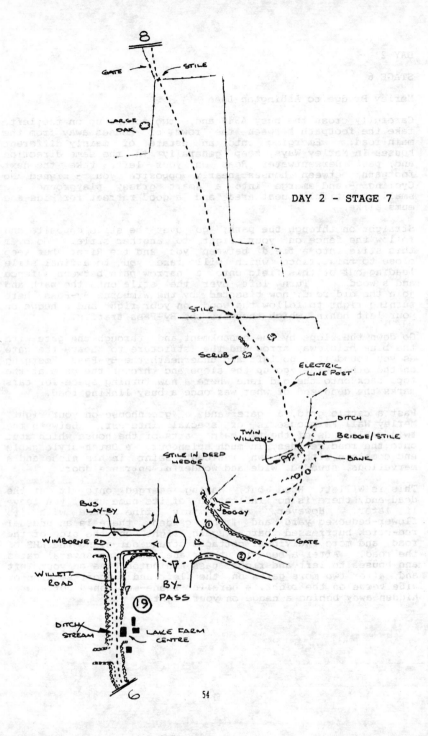

DAY 2 – STAGE 7

54

DAY 2

STAGE 7

Ashington Lane to Eye Bridge

Having joined a ditch alongside the road on your left, keep on
past a LH turning and the Lake Farm Cross Country Centre on
the right and, in 100 yards, our road emerges onto the busy
Wimborne Road opposite a bus lay-by. Turn right and keep to
the pavement. Cross the By-Pass and join the pavement on the
RHS of Wimborne Road opposite. Now, various malevolent
forces may have conspired against your progress in the
intended manner but go and check before taking the
alternative. The problem is a very boggy, uncrossable patch
in the field immediately beyond the stile which you are meant
to use - and I'm mean BOGGY, not just muddy. Firstly, trees
and shrubs which were planted on the wide verge on the
opposite corner when the By-Pass was built have grown together
and hidden the approach to the stile - still signposted
"Footpath to Eye Bridge 3/4 mile". Secondly, if you succeed
in reaching the stile, there is no point in climbing over it
because you will instantly plunge into a wide, straggly morass
of mud and stagnant water. Instead, as recommended by the
Countryside Commission, a small diversion should be made and
you should walk further down the main road towards Wimborne
until you have passed the line of new trees and arrived at a
farm gate into the field behind the trees. Over the gate,
aim for the pair of large willow trees ahead of you and
slightly right, passing between two scrubby hawthorn bushes
and down a slight embankment to reach them. From these
willows, you will see a footbridge over a wet ditch and, if
you had managed to get across the bog after the stile, you
would have come to this spot, anyway.

Cross the footbridge and go over the stile at the other end.
Here, aim for the left of the electric line post in this field
ahead of you and from thence, between scrub bushes, to a stile
in a wire fence in the same general direction. Over this
stile, continue in the same direction, aiming for a distant
large oak which stands on its own behind the left of the two
fences which enclose this very large field.

A very indistinct path meanders across the field towards this
tree and on past it to a stile in the far left corner. Go
over this stile and aim for the footbridge over the River
Stour.

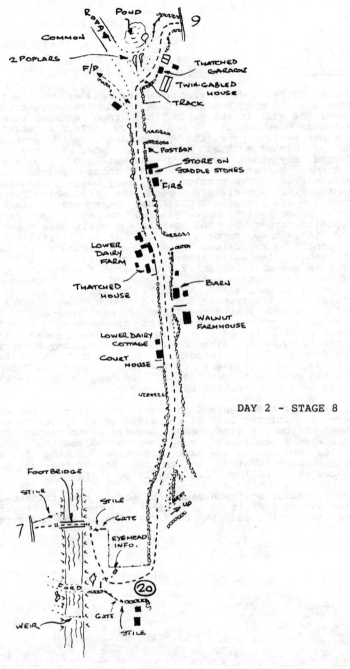

ROAD

COMMON

POND

9

2 POPLARS

F/P

THATCHED GARAGE

TWIN-GABLED HOUSE

TRACK

POSTBOX

STORE ON STADDLE STONES

FIRS

LOWER DAIRY FARM

THATCHED HOUSE

BARN

WALNUT FARMHOUSE

LOWER DAIRY COTTAGE

COURT HOUSE

DAY 2 - STAGE 8

FOOTBRIDGE

STILE

STILE

GATE

7

EYEMEAD INFO.

UP

ORD

(20)

WEIR

GATE

STILE

DAY 2

STAGE 8

Eye Bridge to Cowgrove

The fine timber bridge is an excellent vantage point from
which to observe the coots, moorhens, swans and - again - a
kingfisher, if he comes out to show off his magnificent
plumage.

Also, as you gaze around from here, you can see the Minster
Church of St Cuthburga in Wimborne and the medieval Julian's
Bridge where the Stour veers off to go around the Southern
edge of Wimborne. Across the footbridge, go down the steps
and, passing a stile adjacent to the bridge, walk downriver
for a few yards and then, between timber posts by the Eye Mead
Information board, turn into the gravel car park next to the
River ford. Leave the car park onto the road and turn left.

Cross the road, for safety reasons, and keep straight on, past
the "Pamphill" sign and the turnings which go off uphill on
your right either side of a high-banked and hedged island.
The low hedge on the left gives good visibility across the
low, lush green meadows which accompany the River. A few
yards further on, you pass the Old Court House - a fine,
timbered and restored building which has recently benefitted
from the expert attentions of the National Trust. In fact,
all of the land, roads, farms and houses from here to well
beyond Kingston Lacy belong to the National Trust following a
huge bequest in 1981 before the death of the late Ralph
Bankes.

After Lower Dairy Cottage on the left and Walnut Farm on the
right, you arrive at a group of buildings consisting of the
old thatched farmhouse, barns and outbuildings of Lower Dairy
Farm with a track opposite leading up towards higher grazing
land. The number of individual farms along this stretch is
surprising (Firs farmhouse is next) and just shows how many
farms and families could be supported by the rich grazing and
arable land along the lush edges of the River Stour. The
lower pastures are still best for cattle whilst the chalky
fields higher up provide excellent cereal growing conditions.
Adjacent to the "Firs" is one of the few remaining grain
stores still on its original staddle stones to keep out
marauding rats.

Continuing along the road to Cowgrove Common, you will find a
signed "Footpath" route goes to the left across the common
beside a thatched cottage whilst, with the road continuing
ahead, a track bears off right by a twin-gabled house with a
thatched garage. Take this track, past twin poplars before a
duck pond and follow it between a LH wooden fence and a RH
hedge and bend immediately around to the right.

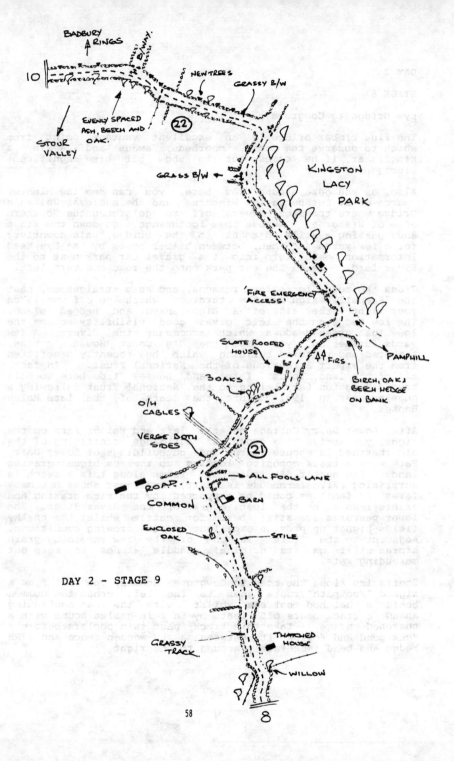

BADBURY RINGS

B/W

NEW TREES

GRASSY B/W

10

EVENLY SPACED ASH, BEECH AND OAK.

STOUR VALLEY

22

GRASS B/W

KINGSTON LACY PARK

'FIRE EMERGENCY ACCESS'

SLATE ROOFED HOUSE

PAMPHILL

FIRS.

BIRCH, OAK, BEECH HEDGE ON BANK

3 OAKS

O/H CABLES

VERGE BOTH SIDES

21

ALL FOOLS LANE

ROAD

BARN

COMMON

ENCLOSED OAK

STILE

DAY 2 - STAGE 9

GRASSY TRACK

THATCHED HOUSE

WILLOW

58

8

DAY 2

STAGE 9

Cowgrove to New Barn Farm

Keep following the grass track with hedges left and right to
another grassy common across which you will see a row of four
pairs of white cottages. Here, a signed footpath goes off
over a stile on your right. Ignore it and keep straight on,
past a fence-protected oak, to a tiled house with a barn at
the rear. Just past the house, a narrow path goes uphill to
the right. This is All Fools Lane which leads up to the fine
cricket pitch, pavilion and beech avenue on Pamphill Village
Green - all still part of the Kingston Lacy Estate. However,
keep on past the bridleway sign to join the road ahead.

Now turn right and keep to the RH side of the road which has
verges on both sides at first. Passing beneath OH electric
cables and by a group of new trees on the right, keep on the
road which now has beech hedges on both sides. After a few
bends and now going slightly uphill, the road verges have
disappeared and so have the ditches, so be careful for 100
yards as you are confined by close beech hedges with a small
pine wood on your right. Soon you reach a sharp RH bend in
the road, with a high bank with a birch, oak and beech hedge
on the RH corner.

Here, keep to the left and turn left by a bridleway sign into
the wide entrance to the bridleway which goes all round the
perimeter of Kingston Lacy Park. Go through the "Emergency
Fire Access" gate after a parking area for a few cars and,
with a verge, a ditch and a hedge on your left, start on the
long bridleway, past the well-kept garden of a small estate
cottage on your right.

All of the great trees on your right are bordering Kingston
Lacy Park and numerous signed gates on the way will remind you
that the estate is very "Private" unless you come in through
the front gates and pay for your admission. Now with grass
up the middle of the track, start slightly uphill and pass
under the branches of a huge beech tree which hangs right over
the bridleway from beyond a ditch on your right. With
ditches, bushes and wire fences alternating along the edges of
the track, go round the RH bend in the track and pass the
"Bridleway" sign where a wide grassy bridleway goes off to
your left and a deep, wide ditch guards the corner. Keep on
to the second "Bridleway" sign and turn left onto the wide
grassy bridleway. On both sides of this track are old and
new ash, oak and beech trees, evenly spaced along the hedges.

Over on the right you can see the heights of Badbury Rings,
the Iron Age hill settlement. Named after Bada, the local
chief of the Durotriges, this hill fort fell to Vespasian in
the early days of his invasion of South-West England which

began with the submission of the Isle of Wight (Vectis) in AD 45, followed soon afterwards by the loss of Hengistbury Head to the invaders. Then, using Badbury Rings as his base, Vespasian moved to take the fortifications at Spetisbury, Buzbury, Hod and Hambledon - all connected with our adventure. Having fortified Badbury Rings, the Romans built a vast network of roads which still reach out into the surrounding country.

Now, after a myriad of farm gates to left, right and centre and a wide grass bridleway going off to your right (along which you can see Badbury Rings) just keep pressing on along the track with fine views ahead into the Stour valley and, on your right, towards the 1 mile long beech avenue on the B3082 Blandford Forum to Wimborne Minster road.

..which goes all round the perimeter
of Kingston Lacy Park - Day 2, Page 59

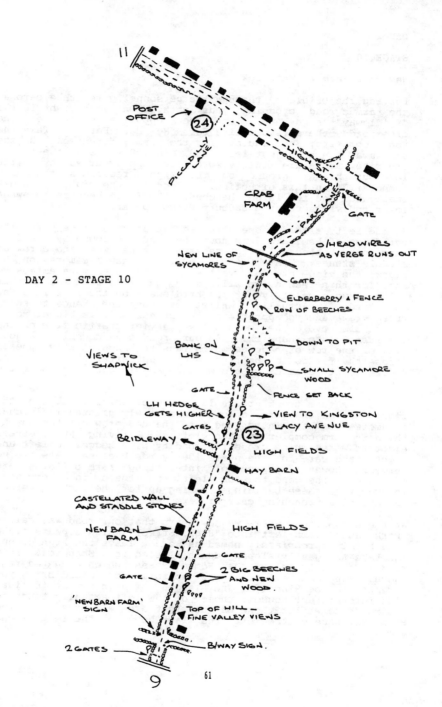

DAY 2 - STAGE 10

11

POST OFFICE

24

PICCADILLY LANE

HIGH ST

CRAB FARM

PARK LANE

GATE

O/HEAD WIRES
AS VERGE RUNS OUT

NEW LINE OF SYCAMORES

GATE

ELDERBERRY & FENCE

ROW OF BEECHES

BANK ON LHS

DOWN TO PIT

VIEWS TO SHAPWICK

SMALL SYCAMORE WOOD

GATE

FENCE SET BACK

LH HEDGE GETS HIGHER

VIEW TO KINGSTON LACY AVENUE

GATES

BRIDLEWAY

23

HIGH FIELDS

HAY BARN

CASTELLATED WALL AND STADDLE STONES

NEW BARN FARM

HIGH FIELDS

GATE

GATE

2 BIG BEECHES AND NEW WOOD.

'NEW BARN FARM' SIGN

TOP OF HILL -
FINE VALLEY VIEWS

2 GATES

B/WAY SIGN.

9

61

DAY 2

STAGE 10

New Barn Farm to Shapwick

Leaving the bridleway through the personnel gate, take care at
the tarmac road crossing your path. On your right is the
"Bridleway" sign and, on the opposite corner of the
crossroads, there is a notice for "New Barn Farm". Take the
road opposite, continuing in the same direction as the
bridleway you have just left and, in 100 yards at the top of
the rise, there are fine views into the Stour valley on the
left but higher ground on the right restricts the view
temporarily in this direction. Soon on the right, at a new
small wood and two large beeches, the field becomes somewhat
lower and views towards Badbury Rings appear.

On the left, after an open-fronted equipment storage barn, the
buildings of New Barn Farm abut the road, followed by the fine
farm house behind a low castellated stone wall and a row of
staddle stones. Arriving at a row of new sycamores on the
right, the view into the valley becomes even more extensive
and, for this reason, we will stay on this road for another
1/2 mile when we arrive at the bridleway on the left in a few
more yards. Actually, whilst we have the chance to enjoy
these views and to appreciate the breeze on this higher road,
we can also avoid the marginally heavier traffic flow on the
lower road into Shapwick. As our road goes downhill, a good
view of the row of beeches which runs to Kingston Lacy appears
across the fields on the right and, just after the small wood
on the right, a track goes down into an old quarry also on the
right.

Just after this track, there is a row of large beeches on the
right and, on the left, a long row of newly planted individual
sycamores has been introduced into the hedgerow all the way to
the next farm complex on the left. Arriving at overhead
electric wires which cross the road by high hedges to left and
right, take care for the next 100 yards because there are no
verges. However, a group of interesting farm buildings are
just around the bend to the left and there is a very wide
forecourt to these buildings, making up for the lack of verges
in case of approaching cars or farm vehicles.

At the crossroads, where we now learn that our road was called
"Park Lane", turn left into "High Street" which appears to be
somewhat inappropriately named as we now leave the high ground
and take the gently sloping downhill road into Shapwick. This
road is actually one of the Roman Roads which emanated from
Badbury Rings and a 1 mile trip up this raod would bring you
directly to the Rings. The length of High Street is lined
with intermittent houses, those on the left actually touching
the roadside whilst those on the right are well back. Passing
Picadilly Lane on the left, the last house on the left is one

of the last surviving village shops and, even if you are fully
provisioned for this journey, go in and buy something -
anything - just to prolong its survival as long as possible.
It's also a Post Office and, at the time of my visit, it was
open daily from 9.00 until 5.30 with lunch from 1.00 to 2.00
except Thursdays and Saturdays when it was open from 9.00
until 1.00. How's that? You don't get this sort of
information from any old guide book. Anyway, after the Post
Office, there is a field on the left and more houses on the
right which take you all the way into the centre of the
village.

Incidentally, Shapwick gets its name from the Saxon "sceap"
meaning sheep and "wic" meaning, as mentioned in the first
part of this Walk, village.

..all the way into the centre of the
village - Shapwick - Day 2, This Page

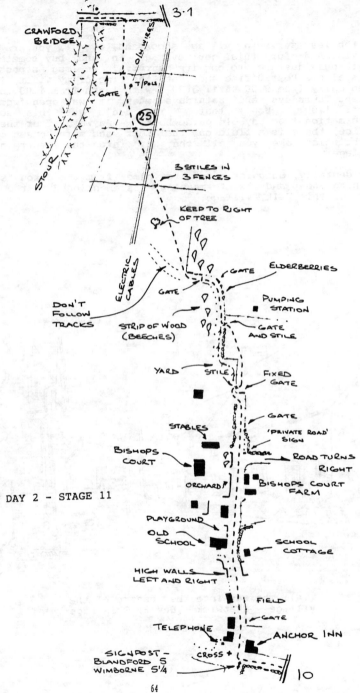

3.1

CRAWFORD BRIDGE

OLD MILES

GATE

T/POLE

(25)

STOUR

3 STILES IN 3 FENCES

KEEP TO RIGHT OF TREE

ELECTRIC CABLES

GATE

GATE

ELDERBERRIES

DON'T FOLLOW TRACKS

PUMPING STATION

STRIP OF WOOD (BEECHES)

GATE AND STILE

YARD

STILE

FIXED GATE

GATE

STABLES

'PRIVATE ROAD' SIGN

BISHOPS COURT

ROAD TURNS RIGHT

ORCHARD

BISHOPS COURT FARM

DAY 2 - STAGE 11

PLAYGROUND

OLD SCHOOL

SCHOOL COTTAGE

HIGH WALLS LEFT AND RIGHT

FIELD

GATE

TELEPHONE

ANCHOR INN

SIGNPOST - BLANDFORD 5 WIMBORNE 5¼

CROSS +

10

64

DAY 2

STAGE 11

Shapwick to Crawford Bridge

Arriving at the crossroads with the Anchor Inn on the RH corner, stop to rest on the stone steps of the village cross. This is a pleasant spot to linger awhile after a busy day's walking but ignore the signpost which says "Blandford 5 miles and Wimborne 5.1/4 miles" because this does not add up to the 14.1/2 miles of walking to which you are currently being subjected and, after the last 1.1/2 miles of on-road walking, you may be a little footsore and weary. We'll soon be off this unforgiving tarmac though and, after a brief visit to the Church of St Bartholomew near the crossroads, take the Blandford direction. Passing houses on right and left sides and between high walls, you arrive at the Old School on the left and the School Cottage on the right. Shapwick is still almost complete, with its Post Office and shop, its village cross, its church by the River and its Inn. Even the old School playground is still there whilst, opposite the School, the school teacher's cottage still has its name displayed evoking images of the dedicated school ma'am tending her hollyhocks on Sundays and her other little flowers during the week. However, I digress - again.

Continue past the School and, on the right, the farm buildings of Bishops Court Farm are situated, after a small field. On the left, high walls protect a fine orchard, followed by Bishops Court farmhouse set back across a lawn with two superb copper beeches against the roadside. Opposite the farmhouse, the road bends right but do not follow the road anymore. Instead, keep on straight ahead, past the "Private Road" sign, for 100 yards with a field on the right and a hedged garden on the left. Arriving at a farm yard on the left, go over the stile in the fence on the right into the field. If the field is full of crops, as it was when I passed through, it may be preferable to stay in the yard and head for the track in the far LH corner instead of going through the field and needlessly damaging the crops, even though the path around the edge of the field should be kept clear for walkers. The sketch map shows how short the alternative path needs to be - only about 100 yards of track - and this would mean that you wouldn't even leave a footprint or get your socks and boots full of wheat or corn ears.

Through the farmyard and on the track, go past the stile on your right, over which you would climb if you went through the field instead, and follow the bend in the track to the left. This bend takes you through a gap in a long, narrow coppice of beech trees and into fine, lush meadowland. On the edge of the wood, go over the farm gate and keep to the wire fence on your right for a few yards. At the gatepost at the end of the fence, a yellow arrow points vaguely in the direction you

should take across the field but a better guide is the
solitary tree in the field. Keep to the right of this tree -
don't follow the tractor tracks - and don't go under the
overhead wires in this first field. This line will lead you
straight to the stile into the second field. You do go
under the overhead wires in this next field to the next stile
into the third field. Now aim for the gate in the far left
of this field because the stile we need next is adjacent to
it.

On your left, the River Stour reappears but, if you go near
it, take care not to alarm any nesting ducks or coots who
favour the reed beds here.

Over the stile into the last field before Crawford Bridge,
don't aim for the bridge itself because the way out onto the
road is over the stile by a gate about 200 yards to the right
of the bridge. Over this stile, our route goes to the right
but firstly we have to go left along the road as far as
Crawford Bridge for a very specific reason but also for
another look at the Stour as it runs along the foot of the
ribbon-developed village of Spetisbury on the A350. The
bridge alone is worth a detour so that we may admire the
nine-arched construction and the four refuges from speeding
carriages, but our primary objective is to carefully observe
the River level gauges.

On our approach into Charlton Marshall in another 3.3/4 miles
on Day 3, the level of the River at this bridge becomes more
than of passing interest because, where the bridleway from
Buzbury Rings crosses the Stour, there is NO bridge. The
Stour has always, since time immemorial, been crossed by a
ford at Charlton Marshall. Don't panic, though. It's
perfectly safe if the water level at Crawford Bridge is about
25.6 m on the scale because, at that level, there is only about
9 to 12 inches of water to negotiate when you get to the ford.
Believe me, I've done it - not without a degree of
trepidation, though, I freely admit. However, the River is
perfectly clear so that you can see the bottom and the way
across is clearly marked with bridleway arrows on either side.
Anyway, you have all night and a couple of bus rides in which
to decide whether to roll up your trousers and wade across or
to keep to the road through Langton Long right into Blandford
Forum - see, there is an alternative but more of that later.
For now, Spetisbury village is on the other side of Crawford
Bridge and bus routes 139 and X13 run through to Blandford and
Wimborne, with the 139 continuing into Bournemouth so, if you
have a penchant for the nightlife between days of more gentle
delights, you could arrive back here for the start of Day 3 in
a complete haze.

..onto the road by the Holy Trinity
Church, Stourpaine - Day 3, Page 86

..onto a walkway above two sluice
gates - Cut Mill - Day 4, Page 102

DAY 3 - INTRODUCTION

Crawford Bridge to Child Okeford

You'll need to be a little fitter for this stage as we have some gradients to tackle; nothing horrendous, but our path goes over Hambledon Hill fort on the last Stage of the Day for some magnificent views over the Stour Valley and to whet your appetite for Day 4. If you don't really fancy the climb when you get there, a level alternative is offered but you'd need to dodge a few tractors or cars if you choose that way.

Anyway, before then, we visit Abbey lands and some lovely churches in the Tarrant valley, a tributary of the Stour. We take off our boots and paddle across the ford through the Stour (Yes! There is another way around this bit if you don't want to get your feet wet - it's good fun, though) and then we wander through Bryanston Estate and Durweston village for a few ghost stories.

We visit the village of Stourpaine and amble along the disused railway line for a while and, after the Iron Age and Roman hill forts of Hod Hill and Hambledon Hill, we finish at Child Okeford, nestling serenely at the foot of Hambledon Hill.

	STAGE	MILES	TOTAL
1	Crawford Bridge to Keynston Hill	2	2
2	Keynston Hill to Littleton	2.50	4.50
3	Littleton to Blandford St Mary	1.50	6
4	Blandford St Mary to Bryanston	1	7
5	Bryanston to Durweston	1.25	8.25
6	Durweston to Hod Hill	1.25	9.50
7	Hod Hill to Child Okeford	2.50	12

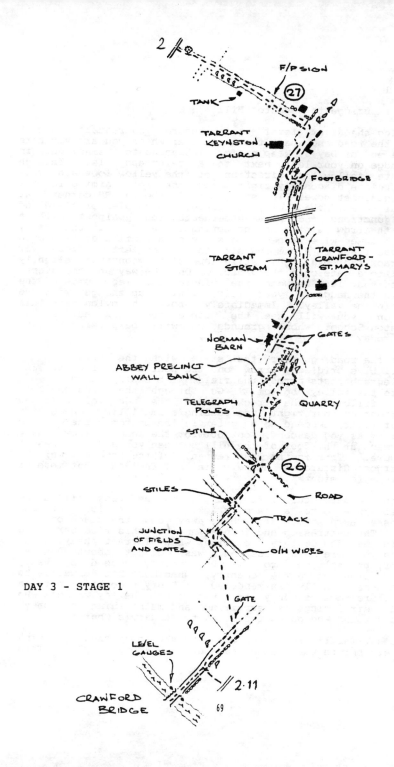

2 //⊗

F/P SIGN

(27)

TANK

ROAD

TARRANT
KEYNSTON
CHURCH

FOOTBRIDGE

TARRANT
STREAM

TARRANT
CRAWFORD-
ST. MARYS

NORMAN
BARN

GATES

ABBEY PRECINCT
WALL BANK

TELEGRAPH
POLES

QUARRY

STILE

(26)

STILES

ROAD

TRACK

JUNCTION
OF FIELDS
AND GATES

O/H WIRES

DAY 3 - STAGE 1

GATE

LEVEL
GAUGES

// 2·11

CRAWFORD
BRIDGE

69

DAY 3

STAGE 1

Crawford Bridge to Keynston Hill

Checking the River level again before you restart, go back
along the road and, past the stile over which you arrived here
at the end of Day 3, keep on for 100 yards to a small gate in
the hedge on your left, next to a telegraph pole. Through
the gate, follow the direction of the yellow footpath arrow
which points diagonally right across the field, aiming for the
first goalpost power line stanchion in the far RH corner. At
the far side of the field, go through a complex of field and
track junctions and pass underneath the goalpost with a
footpath arrow painted on the upright. Head on up the grassy
track between wire fences to a stile by a cantilever gate onto
a tarmac track to a pumping station on the left. Cross over
the track and, over the stile opposite, continue slightly
uphill to a gate onto the road. On the way up this slope,
look to your left between the middle and leg stumps of the
tree in the hedge on your left, lining up the gap with the
pylon in the valley. Immediately above the pylon from this
position, you will see the noble red-brick edifice of
Bryanston School whose grounds we will be passing through
later today.

Across the road, go over the stile with the Dorset County
Council blue bridleway arrow on the post and follow the line
of telegraph posts across the field, with a slope down on your
left to the valley bottom. Go through the gates and bear
right, following the track around the edge of a hedged
embankment on your right and, passing a small limestone quarry
on your right, descend to a gate in the bottom corner of the
field. As you descend, look out for the long, narrow grassy
embankment at the foot of the hill between you and the present
farmhouse. This is the last remnant of the precinct wall of
the largest Cistercian nunnery in all England - but more of
that in a few minutes.

Through the gate, turn left and follow the brick wall to the
smaller gate onto a farm track. Have a look at the
buttressed barn that stretches away down the track on your
left. The buttresses and foundations of this fine barn date
back to the 15th Century, a time when Tarrant Abbey, whose
grounds you are now crossing, was home to about 50 nuns.
However, probably due to the uncertainty caused by Henry
VIII's oppression in the country, when Margaret Russell, the
last abbess, finally surrendered to Henry's commissioners in
1539, there remained only 18 nuns plus the lay workers who
earned their livings by supplying and maintaining the Abbey.
Now turn round and go up the track to St Mary's Church.

This beautiful little church was not the Abbey church, having
been here before the foundation of the Abbey in 1223. This

was the church for the village which had grown up here on the banks fo the Tarrant. Bishop Poore was baptized at the Abbey church, later becoming Bishop of Salisbury in 1217 and being ultimately responsible for abandoning Old Sarum and building the magnificent Salisbury Cathedral. He loved Tarrant Crawford so much that he chose to be buried in the Abbey - the coffin lid with the foliated cross on the North of the altar is believed to be his, having been moved here from the Abbey church. His tomb had been made by Elias of Dereham, the architect of Salisbury Cathedral.

Long before these events, this church already served the community and, even before the Abbey was built, there was a group of nuns living in the "Manse of the Nuns" adjoining the church "having a window looking into it from which the altar was visible". This church was originally dedicated to All Saints at the time of Ralph de Kahaines (see Tarrant Keynston later), about 1170, and he gave it to the Anchoresses (the nuns) together with the manse and the mill.

Inside St Mary's, there are the most wonderful medieval wall paintings, the earliest dating back to the 13th Century, whilst the story recounted on the entire South wall of the nave is that of the martyrdom of brave St Margaret of Antioch. To get the full story, buy the leaflet from the church. This will give you much more architectural detail as well. Now, to continue your walk, leave by the same wrought iron gate by which you entered and turn right along the path which now has the River Tarrant and a line of willows on the left. In a while, the main track goes off right but keep straight on as the path narrows between a wire fence and the stream. 250 yards further on, you arrive at a footbridge across the stream with a large single willow on the left and a waterfall on the right. Over the bridge, turn right on the road and go straight on, past the walled garden and buildings of Manor Farm. Past the church wall on your left, go through the twin gates into All Saints Church, Tarrant Keynston. This is one of eight villages which lie on the Tarrant (Celtic for "liable to flood" and frequently living up to its name). The oldest parts of the church are the tower and the tenor bell. The tower is in the Decorated style and dates back to the 14th Century but the rest of the building was rebuilt in 1852-53 in the old Perpendicular style by T H Wyatt. His name keeps cropping up, but he was the architect for the Salisbury Diocese which controlled parish churches along most of our journey. All Saints was built of flint and ham stone to blend with the old tower and largely in a medieval style similar to the original, old and delapidated building which had to be demolished.

Leaving the church, continue along the road but only as far as the stile and gate about 50 yards away. Here, turn left and go up the concrete track and through the gate onto a gravel farm track with open fields on the left and paddocks on the right. Steadily uphill, pass a yellow arrow by a wood on the right and, as you climb, look back to your right to see the start of the Badbury Rings beeches again. Back on your left, in the far distance, you can see the tower in Charborough Park, the Drax estate, some walls of which were built with stone "liberated" from Tarrant Crawford Abbey after the dissolution.

Now, between two fences, go past a water tank on your left where, to your right, you can see Ashley Wood Service Station across the field. Keep soldiering on (not used to hills, are we?), past a strip of woods on the left and across a track which heads off left, to a solitary tree on the top of Keynston Hill.

The buttresses and foundations..
date back to the 15th Century,
Tarrant Crawford - Day 3, Page 70

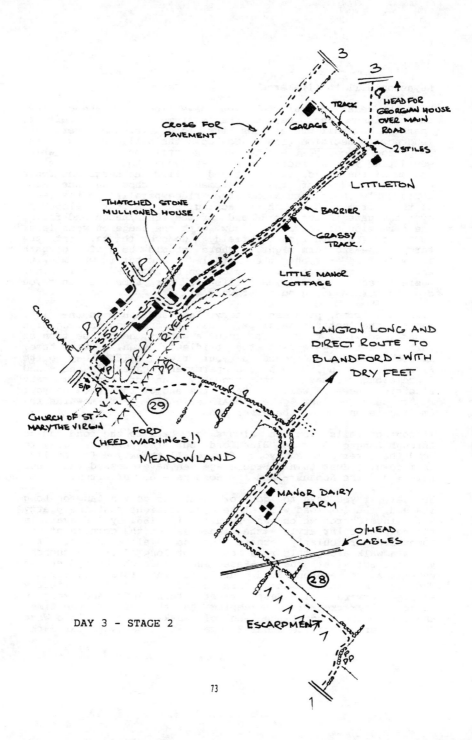

CROSS FOR PAVEMENT

TRACK

GARAGE

3

3

HEAD FOR GEORGIAN HOUSE OVER MAIN ROAD

2 STILES

LITTLETON

THATCHED, STONE MULLIONED HOUSE

BARRIER

GRASSY TRACK.

PARK HILL

LITTLE MANOR COTTAGE

CHURCH LANE

A 350

RIVER

LANGTON LONG AND DIRECT ROUTE TO BLANDFORD - WITH DRY FEET

S/P

29

CHURCH OF ST MARY THE VIRGIN

FORD (HEED WARNINGS!)

MEADOWLAND

MANOR DAIRY FARM

O/HEAD CABLES

28

DAY 3 - STAGE 2

ESCARPMENT

1

73

DAY 3

STAGE 2

Keynston Hill to Littleton

Past the cedar on your right you have fine views ahead across
the lowlands and, beyond the scarpment on the left, to
Charlton Marshall where lies the ford over the River. Not
long now to decision time. Go down the hill, keeping to the
hedge and fence, past a gate and a stile on the right which
would take you indirectly to Ashley Wood Services. At the
bottom of the field, bear left and follow the hedge and fence
along the edge of the escarpment - choosing the most
comfortable sheep path along the ridge parallel to the fence
at the bottom. With ankles aching because of the slope, go
over the gate in the far RH end of the fence/hedge and follow
the direction of the arrow, now with the hedge on your left,
to the far LH corner of the field. Go over the gate into the
tarmac lane and turn right. There should be a DCC footpath
arrow at this exit onto the metalled road but it was missing
when I came out here - it should soon be replaced, if it isn't
there already. And, yes, this is the same road that you
crossed before going on to St Mary's.

Along this road, pass Manor Dairy Farm and house on the right
and, at the foot of the slope, just as the Langton Long sign
comes into view, turn left onto a short, hedged section of
farm track to a gate past the bridleway sign. From here,
follow the hedge and fence on your right all the way to the
River bank, going through two permanent gates in hedge and
fence along the way - and probably one or two temporary
electric fences as well. Near the end of the fence on your
right, past the last gate, bear slightly left towards the
small gate on top of the River bank.

If courage fails, you can always go back to the road and go
through Langton Long to Blandford but it's perfectly easy to
ford the River here and your feet will thank you for cooling
them down. Just think, Bronze Age men have crossed the Stour
here - and the Romans - and the Normans - ad infinitum.

However, if you have to go, or want to go via Langton Long
instead, the low road will take you straight past the pretty
All Saints Church which was rebuilt in 1861 by T H Wyatt in
the perpendicular style - the pinnacles on the corners of the
tower are particularly ornate for so small a church. It's
quite a walk along this road but, not long after the church,
you will arrive at the By-Pass and, through the pedestrian
underpass, to Langton Road until it runs into East Street.
The route map doesn't show this diversion but it's perfectly
straightforward. In East Street, turn left and keep on
through the Market Place, keeping to the left all the time,
and follow the bend at the end of Market Place on into West
Street where, over the Stour Bridge, after Safeways Car Park,

you can meet up with the rest of us, soggy footed, at the junction with Upton Lane on your left.

Now back to the ford. Safely across to the other bank - I hope you aimed for the blue arrow - dry your feet and put your boots back on. Keep straight ahead with an iron-fenced field on your left and the low stone wall of Charlton Marshall's Church of St Mary the Virgin on your right. As you emerge onto the A350 from Poole to Blandford, opposite Church Lane, turn right and go through the gate into the churchyard.

The church was completely rebuilt, all except the base of the tower, in 1713 by Thomas Bastard, whose sons were later to rebuild practically the whole of Blandford after the fire of 1731. The church is considered to be the best example of Georgian church design outside London. The plan is medieval but the inside is pure Georgian, including a tall canopied pulpit, a font similar to that in Blandford's town centre church, clear windows and numerous memorials. Outside, note the fine stone and flint walls and the double-fronted sundial over the porch.

Church Lane opposite is the continuation of the old Roman Road from Buzbury Rings and leads up to Charlton Down and on to Maiden Castle, the major hill fort outside Dorchester. Now continue along the main road, keeping to the RH pavement. Just after a short stretch of wooden fencing on both sides of the road, there are good views over the River valley towards Keynston Hill and there is a weather-vane workshop over the road. Passing a small development of converted farm buildings on your right, turn right down Gravel Lane. On the immediate left hand side of this lane is the fine thatched, stone mullioned Old Dairy Cottage whilst, on the LH bend, the road comes very close to the Stour and a pair of benches offer a short rest.

Before you leave the A350 at Gravel Lane, you really have a choice. The traffic on the main road can be quite threatening and any escape from it is a blessing. However, by turning off here, we only have about 10 minutes before rejoining it and you may prefer to keep straight on. On the other hand, between here and Durweston where the real country tracks and paths start again we aim to get grass under our feet at every opportunity and this diversion is the first of only three such ventures off tarmac in the next five miles. So, continuing with me down the side road, keep straight on past old cottages on both sides of the narrow road until it becomes a grassy track near Little Manor Cottage on the right. Now with hedges and fields on both sides, keep straight on until you meet a stile across your path. Climb over the stile and cross the driveway to a second stile in the wire fence on the other side. Over this stile, you are in a large open field with the A350 running parallel to our path on the LH side of the field. Now aim diagonally left towards the large, Georgian house on the other side of the main road.

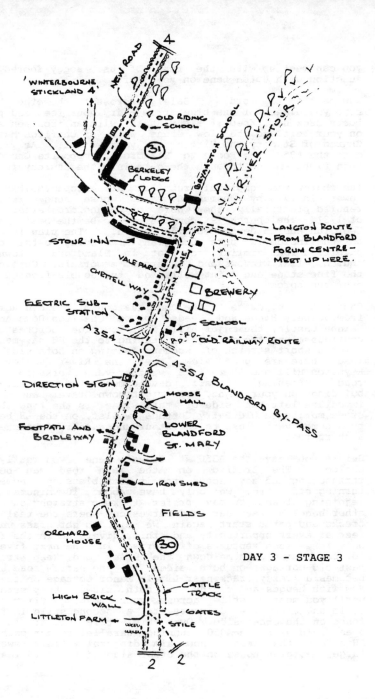

NEW ROAD

4

'WINTERBOURNE STICKLAND 4'

OLD RIDING SCHOOL

BRYANSTON SCHOOL

RIVER STOUR

31

BERKELEY LODGE

LANGTON ROUTE FROM BLANDFORD FORUM CENTRE — MEET UP HERE.

STOUR INN

VALE PARK

CHETTELL WAY

UPTON LANE

BREWERY

ELECTRIC SUB-STATION

A354

SCHOOL

P.O. OLD RAILWAY ROUTE

A354 BLANDFORD BY-PASS

DIRECTION SIGN

MOOSE HALL

FOOTPATH AND BRIDLEWAY

LOWER BLANDFORD ST. MARY

IRON SHED

FIELDS

ORCHARD HOUSE

30

DAY 3 – STAGE 3

CATTLE TRACK

HIGH BRICK WALL

GATES

LITTLETON FARM

STILE

2   2

DAY 3

STAGE 3

Littleton to Blandford St Mary

Keeping in line with the rendered Georgian House, you arrive at a stile with a footpath arrow at the end of the hedge by a pair of farm gates. Opposite you is the entrance to Littleton Farm alongside a high, buttressed brick wall. Cross the road to the pavement and follow the wall which borders the Georgian house. Look out for the wicked draught from the passing heavy lorries and press on towards Blandford St Mary, the sign for which is soon passed after a banked hedge and wooden fence bounding Orchard House on your left. You will have passed a couple of houses on your right backing onto open fields and, after the next two houses, a 6ft wooden fence follows round the next corner of the lane leading right down to Lower Blandford St Mary only, past some converted barns and a church.

However, keep straight on, with the traffic, past a footpath and bridleway sign pointing uphill to your left, a postbox in the wall on the other side of the road and the Moose Hall where the road comes back out from Lower Blandford St Mary.

You will soon be free of all this heavy traffic as, just ahead, you pass the road direction sign before the Blandford Forum By-Pass. Most traffic turns onto the By-Pass and leaves you to wander down Upton Lane opposite into Blandford St Mary. Across the By-Pass, keep to the LH side pavement, past the electricity sub-station. If you look along the line of older trees across the field on your right, you will be able to make out the path of the old railway line as it heads railless and embankmentless towards the remaining section of the old bridge across the Stour 1/2 mile away. Keep straight on, with the school, the sports field and Hall and Woodhouse (Badger Beer) Brewery on your right and with several small housing areas on your left. Towards the end of the road, take special note of the red and grey brick Brook House on your left and also the brick and flint wall on the opposite side of the road. These combinations of building materials typify the style of rebuilding by the Bastard Brothers after the disastrous fire of June 1731 and the centre of Blandford Forum today is the most complete and cohesive surviving example of a Georgian country town in all England. This Walk really does seem to be encompassed by superlatives.

At the end of the road, all those who avoided the ford at Charlton Marshall and carried on through Langton Long will be coming over the River bridge on the right and rejoining us. So, with the large stone entrance lodge to Bryanston School facing you, turn left along the leafy, narrow road on your left between the tree-bedecked green and the row of terrace houses. Keep on until it joins the old Blandford to

Dorchester road in about 100 yards.

Along this side road, you pass the "Stour Inn", strangely the only inn with this name on the entire route, and now cross to the RHS of the old main road, turning left to go past the columned porch of Berkeley Lodge and on to the first turning on your right, New Road signposted to "Bryanston 1.1/4".

The old main road now continues to a dead end because of the new By-Pass whilst, between this and New Road, the centre route goes off into the country to Winterbourne Stickland. In New Road, pass between rows of brick cottages on either side of the road and, with views into the open valley on your left and past the Old Riding School on your right, start a long tarmac, uphill walk. The ivy-clad flint and brick wall accompanying you on your right is the boundary wall of the Bryanston Estate.

Keep on uphill, passing the solitary tree in the hedge on your left and enjoying the views across the wide and open valley.

..the large, stone entrance lodge to
Bryanston School - Day 3, Page 77 .

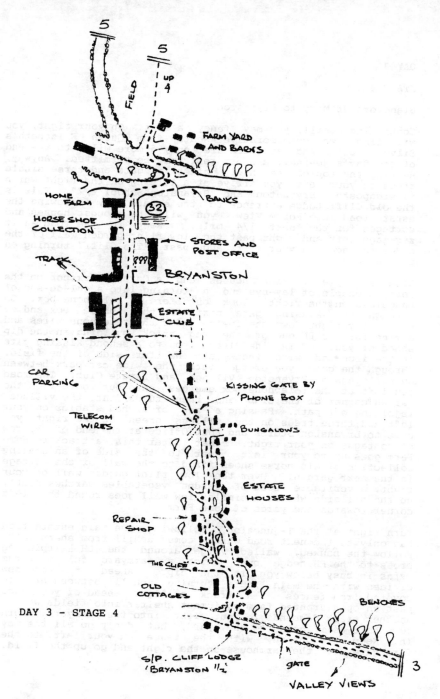

FIELD

5

5

UP 4

FARM YARD AND BARNS

BANKS

HOME FARM

32

HORSE SHOE COLLECTION

STORES AND POST OFFICE

TRACK

BRYANSTON

ESTATE CLUB

CAR PARKING

KISSING GATE BY 'PHONE BOX

TELECOM WIRES

BUNGALOWS

ESTATE HOUSES

REPAIR SHOP

THE CLIFF

OLD COTTAGES

BENCHES

DAY 3 - STAGE 4

S/P. CLIFF LODGE 'BRYANSTON 1½'

GATE

3

VALLEY VIEWS

DAY 3

STAGE 4

Blandford St Mary to Bryanston

Continuing uphill, you may fancy a rest. On your right, you will find two commemorative seats from Queen Elizabeth's Silver Jubilee and, as there are only 6 more miles to the end of the Day's journey, a short rest may be permitted. Anyway, nearing the top of the hill, after a gate and three single trees on your left, you arrive at a turning on the right which is signposted "Bryanston" and "Bryanston School 1/2". This is the old Cliff Lodge entrance to the estate and, following the estate road into Forum View, you will be amongst houses and cottages for the next 1/4 mile. Keep to the road as it zig-zags left and right past the low flint garden wall of the older cottages on your left and past "The Cliff" turning on the RH bend.

After a couple of brick houses and a Garage/Workshop on the left, a couple of lay-bys and a turning into a cul-de-sac of bungalows on the right, look out for a telephone box. Go through the kissing gate next to the 'phone box and go diagonally right down the field, under the telephone wires and aiming for the LH end of the red brick building in the dip ahead of you. This line leads you to a second kissing gate in the iron and wire fence at the far side of the field. Through the gate, you emerge into the wide car park between outbuildings of Bryanston Village and Estate Club. The road you left at the telephone box emerges onto our route from the far RH corner of the Club and then turns into the village, rejoining our path. Passing a row of arched stables on your left and three trees on the village green on the right, you come to Bryanston Stores and Post Office at the end of the row of cottages on your right. Just after this, a track to Home Farm goes up to your left, just to the side of an amazing collection of old horse shoes fixed to the wall of the cottage in the next garden. Over the low flint garden wall on your right, a veritable feast of garden vegetables marches neatly up the hillside whilst a similar low wall goes round the left corner towards the yards of Home Farm.

Turn right at the T-junction, following the main estate road but only to the next road which comes uphill from sharp left. Follow the banked, walled verge around the LH hairpin and cross to the RH hedge over which a farmyard full of large barns is busy below you in the dip. Ahead, the road now divides with the main route turning uphill between bramble covered iron fences. A track straight ahead of you leads past an open-fronted farm equipment shelter into fields whilst another track descends to your right into the farmyard. Turn down here as if going to the yard, but don't go all the way in. Keep straight on, with the fence on your left, to the farm gate with the farmhouse on the right and go up the field.

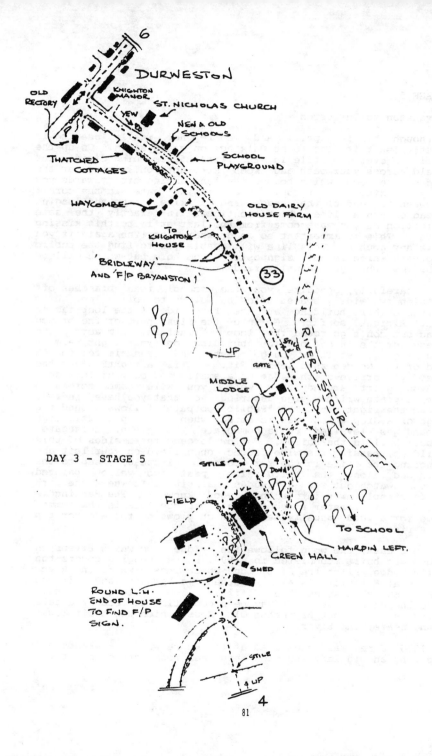

DURWESTON

OLD RECTORY

KNIGHTON MANOR

YEW

ST. NICHOLAS CHURCH

NEW & OLD SCHOOLS

SCHOOL PLAYGROUND

THATCHED COTTAGES

HAYCOMBE

TO KNIGHTON HOUSE

OLD DAIRY HOUSE FARM

'BRIDLEWAY' AND 'F/P BRYANSTON 1'

33

UP

RIVER STOUR

STILE

GATE

MIDDLE LODGE

DAY 3 - STAGE 5

F/P

STILE

DOWN

FIELD

TO SCHOOL

HAIRPIN LEFT.

GREEN HALL

SHED

ROUND L.H. END OF HOUSE TO FIND F/P SIGN.

STILE

UP

4

DAY 3

STAGE 5

Bryanston to Durweston

Although this is uphill and you're not really used to it
(yet), isn't it nice to be walking on grass again. On up the
hill, go over the stile in the wire fence which divides the
field across your path and keep straight on, aiming for the
end of the hedge which bounds the lane arcing back towards you
on your left. Go through the kissing gate in the corner
between the end of the hedge and a wire fence and imagine
ahead of you a line which continues in exactly the same
direction as you have come from the last stile to this kissing
gate. This is important so read that last line again if you
have any doubts. This line will enable you to find the public
footpath which is not signposted from here but which will be
confirmed when you actually find it.

Now, carefully, opposite you the school road branches off
between two widely spaced brick buildings to form a loop which
serves a third building at the far side of the loop facing
you. Alright, so far? Go into the first part of the branch
road but don't go round the loop. Instead, aim across the
grass for the LH end of the building on your right, almost
brushing against it as you go past, and then aim for the LH
end of the wooden shed behind it. Still alright? Past the
shed, you arrive at the edge of a small wood on your left and,
as you skirt around this wood, you will come across a
copper-plate written sign assuring you that you have, indeed,
found the right way. The "Public Footpath" follows around the
edge of a drop which was created when the top of this high
ground was levelled to accommodate the green, corrugated
school hall in the hollow. Follow around three sides of this
building, passing the wire-fenced open field on your left and
ignoring the stile in the far corner. Instead, keep to the
path and, along the third side, past two yellow painted
arrows, watch out for a sudden hairpin left where the path
drops steeply away into a thick wood, known as "The Hanging" -
not for any sinister reason, merely because this is the common
name for a wood, usually beech, which grows on the edge or top
of a ridge.

In this case, the wood follows the ridge upon which Bryanston
House was built, completed in 1894. The Hanging covers the
North ridge whilst the East ridge which runs down to the River
bridge at Blandford is also clothed in hardwood and softwood
trees and is known as "The Cliff". Now, before we descend
into the dark woods, this may be a good time to recount a tale
which is told about Bryanston Old House which was built lower
down, nearer the River.

In 1870, a new maid who lived at the House was awakened one
night by an old lady who came into her room, stood and stared

at her for a while and then went out again. In the morning, the maid asked the housekeeper who the lady was but the housekeeper did not know because they had no visitors to the House at the time. Later the same day, the maid was being shown around the House by the housekeeper when she saw a picture, pointed at it and said, "That's the lady who came into my room last night". Taken aback, the housekeeper told the maid, "That's Aunt Charlotte. She's been dead for years".

On another occasion, during the last illness of Edward Berkeley Portman, the 1st Viscount Portman whose son William built the present House, an old nurse often heard someone walking about and talking in his Lordship's room at dead of night. She went in twice but, on both occasions, found that he was fast asleep. Being asked about this the next morning, Lord Portman did not seem at all surprised and replied, "Oh, that often happens, it's nothing to hurt". After the House was demolished, between his death in 1888 and the building of the present House, the ghost was often seen wandering about the site of the old House. An old woman was heard to say, "Ha, the Portmans won't have any luck now that they've taken the roof off a ghost". And indeed they did not. Following the death of the 2nd Viscount, the family did not live there for much longer. The House was sold off and became Bryanston School eight years later in 1927.

This event was foretold in another strange way at Bryanston. Flocks of white and coloured peacocks were reared here, having eyes on their tail feathers which apparently resembled watermarks on writing paper. It was said that if the peacocks left Bryanston, the Portmans would soon follow. Strangely, after the 2nd Viscount died in 1919, the 3rd Viscount disposed of the peacocks and the House and part of the estate was sold, as we have heard, in 1927. Whilst on matters ghostly, we cannot go deeper into the woods until I have told you that there is talk around Bryanston of a ghostly pack of hounds, the Portman hunt pack, one especially large hound being headless.

Now keep on down the track between largely coniferous trees to the bottom of the steep slope where the track divides. Take the right track and keep on down to join the estate road once more by a yellow footpath arrow which points back up the hill. Emerging onto the road, now with the Stour very close on the right, turn left and follow the road to the stone and flint Middle Lodge, the most Northerly of the estate lodge gates. Through the gate posts, no gates, follow the road straight ahead with open fields now to left and right. The left one spreads uphill to a wood on its crest and the right one flows away, across the Stour, with views to the A350 and to Durweston bridge. Past a gate on the LHS and a stile in the fence on your right, keep straight on past several ancient trees which are just managing to maintain safe anchorage in the frequently flooded meadowland. Soon, a signpost by a farm gate on the left confirms that your footpath has come 1 mile from Bryanston whilst a bridleway purports to head uphill. At the end of that particular field where the bridleway is supposed to pass into the next field, it disappears. I had been considering an alternative way to Durweston with less tarmac underfoot but had to abandon it from that direction.

Anyway, when you're struggling up Hambledon Hill at the end of Day 3, you may look back on this easy road with affection. For now, keep straight on past the high banked, fenced field on your left, the Old Dairy Farm House on your right and the turning up to Knighton House School on your left. Further down the road, you can enjoy the temporary sanctuary of a pavement on your right as it runs alongside the high fence of Durweston School's playing field.

Just after the LH turning into the Haycombe housing estate, you will see the old British Railways Station nameplate for "Stourpaine and Durweston Halt" salvaged and screwed to the wall in the playground. A little later on, we will be passing through Stourpaine and actually walking along part of the abandoned track on its way to the market town of Sturminster Newton. Past the Old School and the New School on your right and a row of thatched cottages on your left, the pavement ends alongside the wall of St Nicholas' Church (closed on school holidays). Note the huge yew tree which grows alongside the church tower. The church was rebuilt in 1847 by P C Hardwick but still manages to retain a rather strange sculpture of St Eloy shoeing a horse by detaching its leg for ease of working. The knight who presumably owns the horse is holding it up so that it doesn't fall over, being partially legless.

Anyway, past the church and Knighton House on your right, a fine brick and flint house and the entrance to "The Old Rectory" on your left, you emerge onto a T-junction. Before leaving this road, however, an "authentic" tale which is told concerns the part of Durweston where now stands the Old Rectory garden. Generations ago, a ghost in the form of a nurse was wont to wander in that part and, if seen by a child, then that child died in the space of one year. An appeal to the bishop caused him to come and to sprinkle Holy Water on the spot and the ghost never reappeared.

Now leave this road opposite the direction sign showing "Bryanston 4.1/4" to your left and "Blandford 2.3/4" to your right. It's a long way round to Bryanston unless you are on the private estate road. Turn right and go down the hill, between a row of cottages on your right and more spaced cottages and a turning off on your left, towards the main road at the foot of the hill.

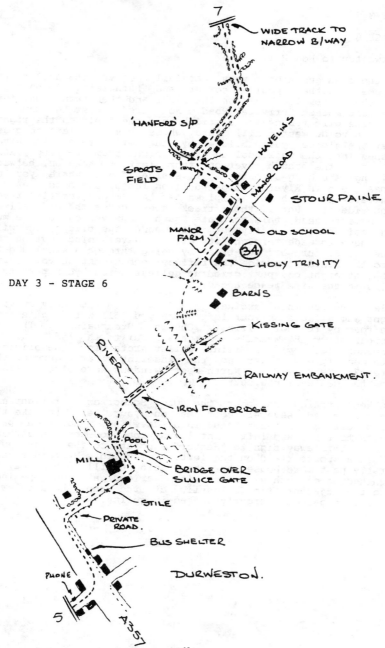

7

WIDE TRACK TO
NARROW B/WAY

'HANFORD' S/D

HAVELINS

MANOR ROAD

SPORTS
FIELD

STOURPAINE

MANOR
FARM

OLD SCHOOL

34

HOLY TRINITY

DAY 3 - STAGE 6

BARNS

KISSING GATE

RIVER

RAILWAY EMBANKMENT.

IRON FOOTBRIDGE

POOL

MILL

BRIDGE OVER
SLUICE GATE

STILE

PRIVATE
ROAD.

BUS SHELTER

PHONE

DURWESTON.

5

A357

85

DAY 3

STAGE 6

Durweston to Hod Hill

At the road junction, very carefully cross the A357 to the
pavement on the opposite corner and turn left. Go past the
bus shelter by the field on the right and then turn right into
the lane marked "Private Road. No Cars". Past two gates in
opposite wire fences and a stile into the field on the right,
keep on to Durweston Mill yard where you turn left to cross
over the sluice gate bridge by the mill race. The River
rushes into the whirlpool on your right from the more placid
waters of the branch river on your left. Keep on, between
railings and hedges, onto a riverside field where you now
cross the main River by a gated, iron footbridge onto a narrow
concrete path which complements the muddy cattle track
alongside it. Until this track goes under the old railway
embankment ahead, this concrete path keeps you out of the mud
and residues (Oh, subtly put) but, under the bridge, you will
just have to wade through it all. Never mind, out on the
other side, turn off the track by going through a kissing gate
into the field alongside the railway embankment on your left.
Keep straight on, past dried up gulleys across your path to a
stile in the wire fence ahead.

This leads you into another field with barns away on your
right and a fence on your left which you follow to a gate onto
the road by the Holy Trinity Church, Stourpaine. This is
another of T H Wyatt's churches, built in 1858 in the
Perpendicular style in flint whilst retaining the original
15th Century West tower and the kneeling vicar figure of the
late 17th Century. The North-West windows were also retained
from the medieval church.

Now keep straight on, past the Old School on your right and
Manor Farm and several cottages on your left, to take the
first left out of Manor Road into Havelins. Carry on, past
houses to right and left, until the road goes over a stream.
Here, a bridleway sign to "Hanford" points to the right, just
before a sports field on the left. Take this Hanford track,
firstly past more houses but then, going uphill, giving way to
high hedges on both sides and with various gates and openings
into the adjacent fields until, at the top, the bridleway
narrows to become a tightly hedged-in gulley.

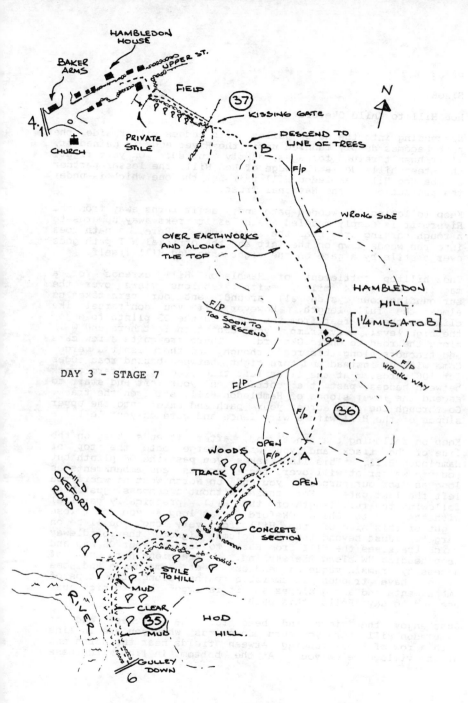

HAMBLEDON
HOUSE

BAKER
ARMS

UPPER ST.

FIELD

4.1

CHURCH

PRIVATE
STILE

(37)

KISSING GATE

DESCEND TO
LINE OF TREES

B

F/P

WRONG SIDE

OVER EARTHWORKS
AND ALONG
THE TOP

HAMBLEDON
HILL

[1¼ MLS. A to B]

F/P
Too Soon TO
DESCEND

O.S.

F/P
WRONG WAY

DAY 3 - STAGE 7

F/P

F/P

(36)

OPEN
F/P

WOODS

TRACK

A

OPEN

CHILD OKEFORD ROAD

CONCRETE
SECTION

STILE
TO HILL

MUD

RIVER

CLEAR

(35)

MUD

HOD
HILL.

GULLEY
DOWN

6

N

DAY 3

STAGE 7

Hod Hill to Child Okeford

Descending into the deep gulley with hedges either side, the
path becomes deeply muddied until the River edge is gained or,
if it hasn't rained for ages, deeply rutted. On your right,
the steep hillside is the edge of Hod Hill, the lesser partner
of the Hod Hill/Hambledon Hill pair but the one which is under
the protection of the National Trust.

Keep following the wooded path and, as it turns away from the
River, it is deeply muddied again as it treks away upwards to
a rough parking area near the roadside. Here, a path goes
into the woods down on the left and the official N T path goes
over a stile by a gate on the right onto Hod Hill itself.

The hilltop settlement of Hambledon Hill extends for a
magnificent 1.1/4 miles, with fabulous views over the
surrounding countryside all around, and our path takes us
almost the full length. However, if you don't feel like
climbing the 400 feet from the road to the OS plinth to enjoy
the high level, airy tramp, you can turn left here and walk
along the road to Child Okeford. There are quite a few cars
and tractors along this road, though, and there isn't a verge.
Come with us instead and turn right, between banked road edges
for 100 yards. At the first left track, go up the farm track
between hedges, past the cottage on your left and start to
ascend the lower slopes of Hambledon Hill, still on the track.
Go through the gate across your path and enter onto the upper
slopes of the Hill with a wire fence and gate on your left.

Keep on following the fence and, after it ends, keep on the
line of the track and you will emerge onto the top of
Hambledon Hill. This line takes you past the OS plinth but
you can wander at will over the ramparts and embankments as
long as, for our purposes, you end up North West of where you
left the last gate. For those without a compass, just keep
following the full length of the Hill, practically parallel
with the road to Child Okeford - as long as you don't lose
sight of this side of the Hill for very long, you'll be on
target. Just beyond the OS column, ignore the bridleway
which traverses the Hill from East to West on your OS map and
keep heading NW along the skyline. Directions here must, of
necessity, remain vague as endless feet, some human and some
ovine, have trodden innumerable paths along the tops of
embankments and along slopes so it is impossible to pick just
one and to say "Follow this path".

Just enjoy the views and head for the farthest end of
Hambledon Hill where you turn downwards when you are in line
with a row of trees running between fields near the North end
of the village below you. At the bottom, in line with these

trees, go through a kissing gate onto a path between the hedge
and trees on your left and a wire fence on the right. Keep
going downwards with the field on your right, to go over a
stile by a gate onto a track by a "Private" stile and a house
on your left.   Go into Upper Street ahead and turn left
opposite Hambledon Cottage.

Passing the fine Georgian Hambledon House on your right,
continue down Upper Street, with houses on both sides, until
you reach the junction with the village cross in the centre,
the "Baker Arms" on the right and the lane to St. Nicholas'
church on your left.

Now, catch your bus or take your car and we'll meet up here
again in the morning.

I know that everybody has gone over Hambledon Hill on the way
here, so all mileages will assume this to be true. Total
mileage to here will ignore the short cut along the lane - so
we now stand at 37.1/4 miles from Mudeford.

...and we'll meet up here again in the
morning - Child Okeford - Day 3, This Page

DAY 4 - INTRODUCTION

Child Okeford to Wyke

This is a completely different Day - no more hill forts to climb - we're on altogether flatter country now as the Stour meanders from one pretty Dorset village to another throughout the whole of Day 4. We cross the River on at least six occasions and walk right by its edge many times before nightfall. Whereas we were forced to lose contact with the River over several periods on Day 3, this section seldom wanders very far away.

Quite early on, we go through the market town of Sturminster Newton so you can stock up with food - and thirst will not be a problem either as we go past five inns and there are optional detours to at least another two. Balancing the secular, we visit five lovely churches, again with possible detours to another four. There are a few more tales of ghosts and witches whilst we go past many watermills, all powered by our River.

All in all, if this section is a little longer than the previous three, there is much variety, it is quite level and there are many pastoral delights.

	STAGE	MILES	TOTAL
1	Child Okeford to Newmans Drove	1.75	1.75
2	Newmans Drove to Fiddleford	2.75	4.50
3	Fiddleford to Sturminster Newton	1.25	5.75
4	Sturminster Newton to Hinton St Mary	1.25	7
5	Hinton St Mary to Yardgrove Farm	1.75	8.75
6	Yardgrove Farm to Marnhull	1.50	10.25
7	Marnhull to Fifehead Magdalen	1	11.25
	+ Fifehead Magdalen to West Stour	(0.50)	(11.75)
	OR		
	+ 7a Fifehead Magdalen to West Stour		
	via Stour Provost	1.50	12.75
8	West Stour to Nations Road	2	(13.75)
			14.75
9	Nations Road to Wyke	1.50	(15.25)
			16.25

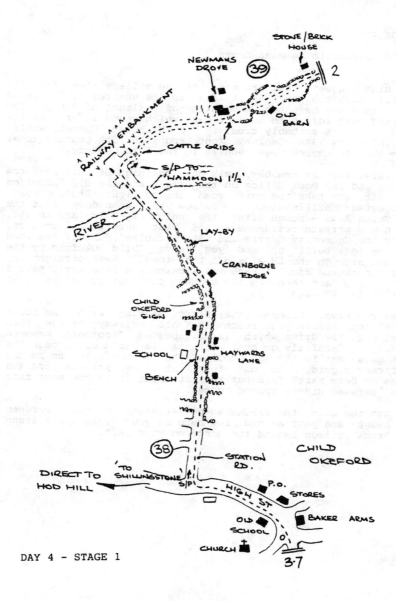

STONE/BRICK HOUSE

NEWMANS DROVE

39

2

OLD BARN

RAILWAY EMBANKMENT

CATTLE GRIDS

S/P TO 'HAMMOON 1½'

RIVER

LAY-BY

'CRANBORNE EDGE'

CHILD OKEFORD SIGN

SCHOOL

HAYWARDS LANE

BENCH

38

STATION RD.

CHILD OKEFORD

DIRECT TO HOD HILL

'TO SHILLINGSTONE'

S/P

HIGH ST

P.O.

STORES

OLD SCHOOL

BAKER ARMS

CHURCH

3·7

DAY 4 – STAGE 1

91

DAY 4

STAGE 1

Child Okeford to Newmans Drove

Hutchins suggests that the name of the village stems from its "chill" situation but, as it lies in the shelter of Hambledon Hill, this may have been something of a flight of fancy. The Okeford part refers to ancient oaks which stood in or near the ford - this is probably true. St Nicholas' Church, whilst retaining its 13th Century font and the 15th Century tower from the old church, was rebuilt in the 19th Century.

Now, starting the new Day, walk down the High Street, past the Stores and the Post Office on the right and the Old School on the left, and take the next road on the right, Station Road, signposted "Shillingstone". Follow this road down, past the old Union Arms - named after the union with Ireland in 1801 but now a private residence - and past several cul-de-sacs. After the Community Centre and St Nicholas' School, the road becomes less built up and you leave Child Okeford by the village sign on the LH side of the road. Keep straight on, past "Cranborne Edge" (Cranborne stretches a long way), past a small lay-by and then, as the hedges give way to fences, keep over to the RH side.

Cross the River bridge (the first meeting with the Stour today) and, before you reach the old railway bridge, turn right onto the drive which is signposted "Footpath Hammoon 1.1/2". Carefully go over the cattle grid or through the farm gate next to it and follow the tarmac drive on to the next cattle grid. Do not turn into the private yard and barns of Bere Marsh Farm but keep straight on to the next farm gate, between widely spaced hedges.

Through the gate, the track keeps straight on, still between far hedges and past an old, low barn on your right and a stone and brick cottage behind the hedge on your left.

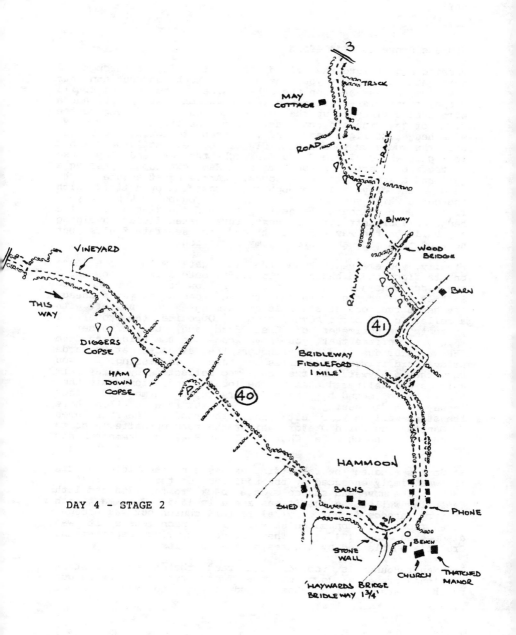

3

MAY COTTAGE

TRACK

ROAD

TRACK

B/WAY

RAILWAY

WOOD BRIDGE

BARN

VINEYARD

THIS WAY

DIGGERS COPSE

HAM DOWN COPSE

41

'BRIDLEWAY FIDDLEFORD 1 MILE'

40

HAMMOON

BARNS

SHED

S/P

PHONE

DAY 4 - STAGE 2

BENCH

STONE WALL

CHURCH

THATCHED MANOR

'HAYWARDS BRIDGE BRIDLEWAY 1¾'

DAY 4

STAGE 2

Newmans Drove to Fiddleford

Passing a gate into the field on your left, go through the next gate in front of you where the track runs out and into the wide, grassy area on the other side. Here, on the uphill slope, there is a track going down on your right and a wire-fenced vineyard up the slope to your left. Keep to the right of the vineyard and, past this, the track becomes clear with hedges to right and left. Keep following the route, near the woods on your right, Diggers Copse, until you reach a farm gate ahead of you. Go through the gate and keep close to the woods, still on your right, Ham Down Copse, passing a gate and a stile into these woods. Arriving at a gate in the hedge ahead of you, go through and cross the open field, with the copse which you can see ahead of you being kept on your right. Go on through the next gate and now keep near to the hedge on your left for the next three gated fields, avoiding any bulls on the way - I met three, in separate fields, but none of them made any moves in my direction

Finally, you emerge through the last gate, with a wire fence on its right and a hedge on its left, onto a farm track which the hedge continues to accompany. Follow this hedge and turn left at the junction with the tarmac road a few yards ahead. The hedge runs out at a series of farm gates on your left with a collection of barns beyond them. Opposite, the stone wall protects the perimeter of East Farm and, on the corner, a signpost confirms that you have come on the bridleway from "Haywards Bridge 1.3/4" although the signpost at Haywards Bridge said it was 1.1/2 miles to here. In passing, did you know that a hayward was the man who collected any stray farm animals and delivered them to the local pound, from where they had to be collected by their owners upon payment of a fee? Anyway, I'm digressing again. At the road junction where the stone wall on your left ends, the road to the right goes to Manston and Child Okeford whilst the road opposite leads to a convenient bench, the Church of St Paul and Hammoon Manor House.

St Paul's escaped the rebuilding excesses of the Victorian era and was simply enhanced by the addition of the bell turret in 1885. The nave and chancel date back to the 12th and 13th Centuries whilst the pulpit was added in 1635. The smart 15th Century reredos is not original to this church but was brought here from a stonemason's yard in London where it was discovered in 1945. The stone carving depicts the Crucifixion flanked by figures of the Apostles.

The Manor House is roofed with reed thatch and has stone mullioned arched windows of the Tudor period. The unique porch, a later addition, has ringed baroque columns on either

side of the arched opening similar to those on Ruben's house
in Antwerp (but I bet you knew that already). Hammoon is
named after William de Moion who "brought 47 knights to the
Battle of Hastings".

Anyway, enough of that, you'll be wanting to get on.

Press on down the road to the left of the one on which you
arrived in Hammoon, past the telephone box on your right and,
at first, with houses on both sides of the road. Passing
several gates in the hedges to left and right and past the
high banks bordering the road, you soon arrive at a gravel
track which goes off to your right, signposted "Bridleway
Fiddleford 1". Take this track, with a wire fence on the left
and a hedge on the right, to the farm gate ahead. Through
the gate, follow the track which turns first left and then
right until the hedge on the right ends at a farm gate and a
wire fence with a barn ahead of you, just off the track.

Go left through the gate into a very long field with a fence,
a hedge and some trees on your left. Aim for a spot in the
hedge on the far side of the field approximately 25 yards from
the far LH corner and, on the way across, you will eventually
be able to make out a gate in the hedge. Through the gate,
cross a 4ft wide wooden bridge over a small stream which
leads into a narrow field. Cross this field towards a gate
in the hedge behind which runs the old railway track from
Stourpaine and Durweston Halt to Sturminster Newton.

Go up onto the embankment after the bridleway arrow, turn
right and follow the line for about 100 yards. When the
track emerges from being hedged-in on both sides into an open
field, it continues straight on but you have to leave it here
and turn left to follow the hedge clockwise around the LH edge
of the field until you meet the tarmac road at a wide opening
in the end of the hedge.

Bear right onto the road and follow it, between old hedges,
past Fiddleford Mushrooms and May Cottage on your left and a
farm track going off between hedges an your right.

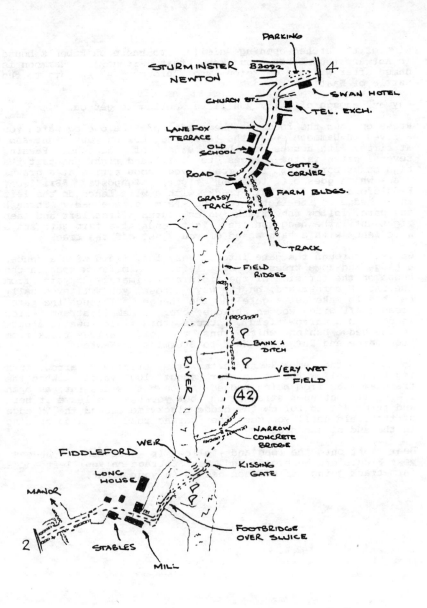

PARKING

STURMINSTER
NEWTON   B3092   4

SWAN HOTEL

CHURCH ST.   TEL. EXCH.

LANE FOX
TERRACE
                OLD
                SCHOOL
ROAD   GOTTS
                        CORNER

                        FARM BLDGS.

GRASSY
TRACK

                        TRACK

            FIELD
            RIDGES

                    BANK &
                    DITCH

            RIVER   VERY WET
                         FIELD

                    42

                    NARROW
                    CONCRETE
WEIR   BRIDGE

FIDDLEFORD
        LONG   KISSING
        HOUSE   GATE

MANOR

    2   FOOTBRIDGE
                        OVER SLUICE
        STABLES

            MILL

DAY 4 - STAGE 3

DAY 4

STAGE 3

Fiddleford to Sturminster Newton

Go past the stile with the "Footpath" sign in the hedge on the
right and cross the stream which runs under the road. Now the
road turns sharply to the left at a sign for "Fiddleford
Manor". Keep straight on between a RH hedge and a LH fence,
through a gate into Fiddleford Mill yard by a sign which
proclaims "Uvedale Limousin Herd" - and keep an eye out for
any of them when you cross the meadows between here and
Sturminster Newton. In the Mill yard, go under the arch
which crosses the path and note the medieval plaque on the
wall to the right. Follow the fenced path round to the left,
past the headwaters on your left and the downriver,
sluice-generated turbulence on the right. Following the
concrete path across the small, wooded island, cross the weir
bridge and pass the "Beware of Snakes" sign in the tree on
your right. I didn't see any, but let's not even think about
it.

Anyway, go through the kissing gate and bear left to the hedge
facing you and go over the narrow concrete bridge into the
long, wet field which runs between the River on your left and
a hedge and bank on your right. Here, I had to divert away
from the path to get past a rather large bull in the company
of several wives. When I say I diverted from the path, this
doesn't mean to imply that it was very clear in the first
place. Depending upon recent usage and the length of the
meadow grass, it may be perfectly clear, failing which it
generally aims straight fot the gap in the distant wire fence,
positioned near the RH hedge, although it isn't really
discernible until you get much nearer to it. Through the gap,
just keep straight on, nearer the hedge now, to a gate and
stile in the far RH corner of the (now) fence.

Go over the stile in the fence into the field and keep
following the vague path, quite near the river now which has a
steep bank on its far side but is low and boggy on this side.
A series of field ridges on your right brings you to the far
side of the field where the wire fence goes down to the River
edge and a gate and stile lead into a hedged hollow-way.
Ignore the farm sheds and the track which goes to them on your
right and head on down the grassy track until you come out,
between houses, onto the tarmac road at the end. This is
Penny Street where you turn right and begin to walk uphill
towards the town.

At Gotts Corner, the fine, tall, stone-built and buttressed
building on the LH corner is the Old School, the entrance
gates being further up on the LH side. Vine House, opposite
the School, is the house where the boy William Barnes, the
greatest ever Dorset dialect poet, was given his first job. He

was only twelve but solicitor Thomas Henry Dashwood was so impressed by Barnes' commendation from his school that he took him on as a clerk. Barnes' achievements academically (his literary works already known nationally, if not internationally) included not only Latin and Greek but seventeen other languages as well.

The LH raised pavement turns off round the corner towards the Church of St Mary, Sturminster Newton. This is a larger church than those already visited which, although largely rebuilt in 1827, managed to keep its 15th Century nave and its North and South aisles. The tower is also of the 15th Century but has been much restored. The old wagon roof of the nave is of special interest and you should not leave without admiring the workmanship.

The name of the town, when broken down into its constituent parts, is almost self-explanatory. Newton, or New Town, is a separate hamlet on the South of the causeway and the bridge between it and Sturminster on the North. Of Newton Castle, little except the mound still remains, near the River opposite the bridge. The medieval bridge has a ten-arch span, widened in the 17th Century and lengthened over adjoining wetland in 1825. "Stour" - the River and, the last piece of the jigsaw, "Minster" - the Church complete our disection of Sturminster Newton.

Now, past the church turning, keep straight on and then bear right into Market Square - the market is not held here anymore though. The Market, held on Mondays, is further on in Station Road. However, whilst here, you cannot help but notice that Sturminster Newton (or just "Stur" to the locals) is crammed with pubs, restaurants and hotels - just the place to come back to at the end of today.

Before you leave, there is a tale around here concerning two old spinsters who were thought to be witches. They lived in a cottage near the River below the church at the turn of the century, earning a living, just, making rush mats and hassocks. Their practices included hanging a bottle with frogs' entrails and a bullock's heart stuck with pins up the chimney - to protect the house from evil spirits so, perhaps, the spinsters were as cautious of witches as other peaople were of them. Anyway, at some time, they seem to have believed that a local school-master had bewitched them and the only way to break the spell was to draw his blood. They managed to accomplish this by scratching him with a pin when they passed him in the street.

In no way connected with this incident, they were found dead together in the snow near Hayden Farm, Plummer, about a mile outside Sturminster Newton and, until recent years, two crosses marked the spot in an adjacent hedge.

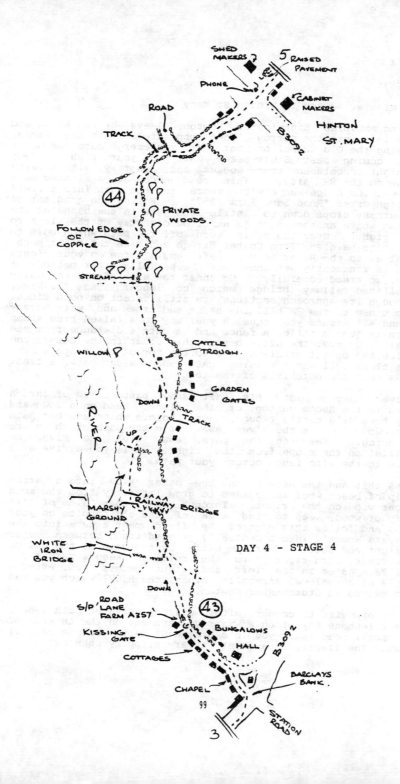

SHED
MAKERS

5 RAISED
PAVEMENT

PHONE

CABINET
MAKERS

ROAD

HINTON
ST. MARY

TRACK

B3092

44

PRIVATE
WOODS.

FOLLOW EDGE
OF
COPPICE

STREAM

WILLOW

CATTLE
TROUGH.

GARDEN
GATES

DOWN

TRACK

UP

RIVER

RAILWAY BRIDGE

MARSHY
GROUND

WHITE
IRON
BRIDGE

DAY 4 — STAGE 4

DOWN

ROAD
S/P LANE
FARM A357

43

BUNGALOWS

KISSING
GATE

HALL

COTTAGES

B3092

BARCLAYS
BANK.

CHAPEL

STATION
ROAD

99

3

DAY 4

STAGE 4

Sturminster Newton to Hinton St Mary

Having explored Sturminster Newton, leave by the B3082 and turn left into the narrow "Row" opposite Station Road where, passing the Old Chapel on your left, you emerge onto the wider road coming past Sturminster Hall on your right. Keep straight on between town houses and, shortly, with a beech hedge on the RH side. This road ends at a kissing gate between the hedge and a wire fence and the path into a field is signposted "Road Lane Farm A357". Follow the gradient of the grassy slope down to a stile and gate in the hedge at the bottom where another path joins from directly up the slope to your right. Over the stile, turn off the path which goes to the white-painted, iron Colber Bridge and take the right path, parallel to the River on your left and a hedge on your right. This is frequently wet underfoot, especially after periods of rain, so tread carefully. Go under the arch of the partially demolished railway bridge which no longer spans the River although its approach sections are still intact on both sides. Keep close to the RH hillside hedge and trees and, with marshy ground all around you, squelch your way to a fallen tree stump which is just a stile, a fence and a gate's distance from the River. Go over the stile beyond this stump in the corner and follow the uphill gradient path to the top of the slope where, by a block wall and a kissing gate and a wider gate, a track leads into the outskirts of the town.

However, keep on past this exit and, past a row of garden gates in the hedge on top of the slope, head on a downward tack towards a cattle trough, just before which another path heads down towards the River, away from the path which we are following. Keep on the path, away from the River and parallel to the slope from the right, until you arrive at a stile in the wire fence across your path.

Cross this and the stream on the other side into a narrow strip of beech wood which seem to grow laterally from the much larger wood on the right. Through the other side of this strip of wood, keep to the edge of the old coppice on your right and follow this edge of the field, past a gate into the "Private Woods", into a centrally-grassed track between hedges to right and left. Over the stile by the gate at the end of this track, turn right onto the road and keep straight on, past farm gates in the left and right hedges and, after a couple of bungalows, carefully cross the B3092 which you had left behind in Sturminster Newton.

On the opposite LH corner, after workshop units on both sides, is a telephone box, then a raised pavement on the LH side of the uphill road leads you into Hinton St Mary - but be careful because the flagstone pavement is very slippery when wet.

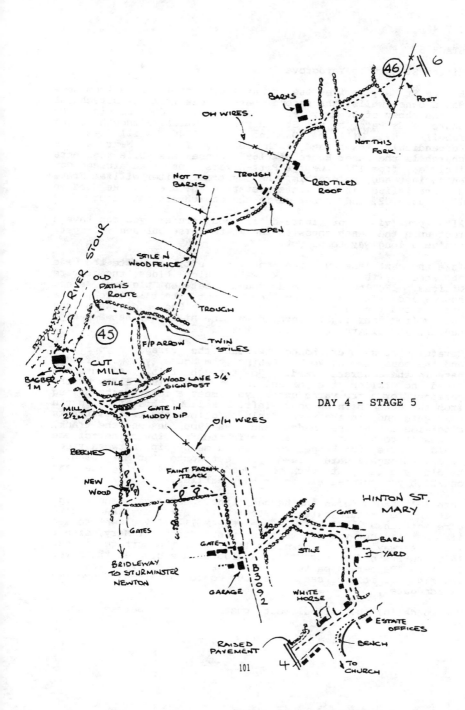

46

6

BARNS

O/H WIRES.

POST

NOT THIS FORK.

NOT TO BARNS

TROUGH

RED TILED ROOF

OPEN

STILE N WOOD FENCE

RIVER STOUR

OLD PATH'S ROUTE

TROUGH

45

F/P ARROW

TWIN STILES

BAGBER 1M

CUT MILL

STILE

WOOD LANE 3/4' SIGNPOST

MILL 2½M

GATE IN MUDDY DIP

O/H WIRES

DAY 4 - STAGE 5

BEECHES

FAINT FARM TRACK

HINTON ST. MARY

NEW WOOD

GATE

BARN YARD

GATES

GATE

STILE

BRIDLEWAY TO STURMINSTER NEWTON

B 3 0 9 2

GARAGE

WHITE HORSE

ESTATE OFFICES

RAISED PAVEMENT

BENCH

TO CHURCH

4

101

DAY 4

STAGE 5

Hinton St Mary to Yardgrove Farm

Hinton St Mary derives the first part of its name from some Saxon owner whilst the second part comes from its attachment to the Abbey of St Mary at Shaftesbury. Go and visit the church - St Peter's, not St Mary's - which, although it was rebuilt by William Osborne in 1846, still has its Perpendicular tower and 12th Century font. Next to the church is the Manor House of 1695 whose erstwhile residents included, from 1929, George Pitt-Rivers, the famed archaeology enthusiast and, before him, the mystical writer William Freke who specialized in the interpretation of dreams. He died in 1744, aged 82, and is buried in the churchyard next door.

After your visit, or instead if you prefer, you can have a rest upon the bench opposite the White Horse but don't forget, you've a long way to go yet.

Take the next lane but one on the left, opposite the wide entrance in the high brick wall which hides the Estate Offices. Follow this road round, between pleasant stone houses and, after a yard on your right, bear left to pass a paddock and then a stile on your left. Soon, joining a lane coming from your right, turn down the hill and, between high hedges, you arrive once more at the B3092.

Carefully cross over and go between the garage on your left and the house facing you. Behind the house, you will find a gate in the concrete yard. Go through this gate into the field and follow the direction of the blue arrow on the gatepost for a few yards until you meet a faint track coming from the dutch barn on your left. Follow this track to the next gate and, in the next field, follow the tractor tracks clockwise around the hedge and, as you descend the track, follow it round until you arrive in the far, low corner of the field. Here, the hedges meet in a muddy dip, between trees which, through a gate, lead you out onto Cut Mill Lane. A bridleway sign points back to "Wood Lane 3/4" being the lane on which you entered Hinton St Mary earlier.

Turn left and go down the hedged lane, past a gate and a sign pointing to "Sturminster Newton Mill 2.1/2". I know we've done more than 2.1/2 miles since the Mill (if you went to see it, that is) but you did want to visit Hinton St Mary, didn't you? Anyway, keep on down the lane, past the cottage on your left, to its end at Cut Mill. A footbridge crosses the River Stour to "Bagber 1" on the left side of the Mill whilst, to the right of it, you can walk out onto a walkway above two sluice gates.

The wonderful Dorset dialect poet, William Barnes, who I

briefly mentioned on your approach into Sturminster Newton, was born in Bagber in 1801 and he learned to swim in the Stour by a bed of water lilies (clotes). It would be nice to think that it could have been near to this spot - there are dozens of water lilies in the calm water above the sluice gates in summer.

The old path from here led upriver for a few yards before going over the fence on the right and then uphill but this has now changed so - go back up the lane and past the gate where you came out onto Cut Mill Lane. Up the lane a little further, go past a farm gate on your left and, in another 100 yards, go left at the footpath post and over the stile beyond the banked hedge. In the field on the other side of the stile, turn right for only a few paces and then follow the RH hedge all the way to its end where you turn right in the far corner by a post with a "Footpath" arrow on it. In this next field, keep close to the LH hedge and then go over the twin stiles a few yards up in this hedge.

Over these, follow the line of the wire fence on your right.

From here, and also from the previous fields, you have views over the lush dairy and arable fields of this special part of North Dorset but, when I came this way, the whole area seemed to be overrun with rabbits - not just a few, a small plague.

Anyway, go over the stile in a short section of wooden fence facing you and follow the path between the wire fence on your right and some trees, behind which lurks a small pool, on your left. In a few yards, you are confronted by two stiles. Don't go straight on but take the RH one, then follow the line of the hedge on your right aiming generally for the red-tiled roof ahead of you. Past several openings in the hedge and past a water trough on your left, you will join a well-worn dirt track which you follow into the cluster of farm buildings with Yardgrove Farmhouse on your right.

Go round to the right after the house and descend to the tarmac lane. Across the lane you will find a stile in the hedge but it's almost hidden enough for you to miss it. Go over this stile and follow the direction of the LH of the two arrows. This keeps you to the LH edge of the field against the hedge and you soon come to another stile in the corner. Cross the stile and aim just to the left of the overhead cable post in the field in front of you.

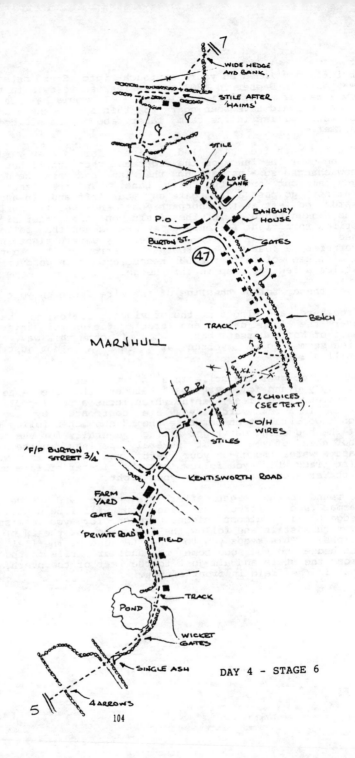

7

WIDE HEDGE
AND BANK.

STILE AFTER
'HAIMS'

STILE

LOVE
LANE

P.O.   BANBURY
                        HOUSE

BURTON ST.   GATES

47

                        BENCH

TRACK.

MARNHULL

                        2 CHOICES
                        (SEE TEXT).

                        O/H
                        WIRES

                STILES

'F/P BURTON
STREET 3/4'

                KENTISWORTH ROAD

FARM
YARD

GATE

'PRIVATE ROAD   FIELD

                        TRACK

POND

                WICKET
                GATES

        SINGLE ASH   DAY 4 - STAGE 6

5   4 ARROWS

104

DAY 4

STAGE 6

Yardgrove Farm to Marnhull

Across this field you will see a post which carries no less
than four DCC arrows.   Go straight past this post to a double
stile which is next to a solitary ash tree by the wire fence.
This stile has another three arrows but keep to the RH of the
field and follow the hedge down to two wicket gates on the
right edge of a duck pond.   Here, we join a Private Road with
pedestrian access, so continue thoughtfully past a few houses
on either side until you emerge onto a busier road just past
the "Private Road" sign and a farmyard on your left. Cross
the road carefully to a footpath sign on the opposite LH
corner of Kentisworth Road.   The sign points through an estate
of bungalows to "Burton Street 3/4".

Follow Kentisworth Road to its end and, past the RH
manouevring area, you will find an alley between fences and
the side of a house. At the end, a stile by a gate takes you
into a field which you go straight across to a stile in the
wire fence and hedge facing you.

In the next field, keep to the LH hedge, past a horse trough
and under overhead electric cables until you reach an opening
between the hedge and a wire fence continuing in the same
direction.   The "Footpath" post tells you nothing, but you
have two choices here.   If you go through the opening in the
fence and head diagonally down the slope to the trees and the
RH end of the hedge at the bottom, you will come to a stile
leading into the woods.   Don't go over the stile but turn at
right angles and go back up the slope to a stile in the top
corner of the field.   (Silly, but it's on the Definitive Map
and the second way isn't).   However, for the second choice -
back at the opening and the "Footpath" post, keep straight on
without going through the opening and keep to the wire fence
on your left until you come to another stile which is also
marked "Footpath" on the other side - no yellow arrows, unlike
the one next to it.   Go over either stile onto the lane and
turn left.

Follow the lane down, past another tempting bench on the
right, and then, with houses to right and left, you arrive at
a junction of roads in the village of Marnhull.   Our lane is
now revealed to be Sackmore Lane and the road to our left
which heads into the Marnhull shops is the "Burton Street"
signposted at the bungalow estate.   There is a Post Office
and a telephone box opposite for anyone wishing to call for
help before the end of Day 4 but try not to give in just yet.
We still have a couple of pubs to go past before the end of
today, so a little sustenance is always available later.
Whilst here, though, we cannot leave Marnhull, which claims to
be the largest village in Dorset, without learning a little

about the area.   Perhaps you might like to go back to that
last bench and have a little read.

In the Rev John Hutchins "History and Antiquities of the
County of Dorset", we find that Marnhull stands "surrounded
nearly on three sides by the River Stour which rises from
seven wells or springs at what is commonly known as Stourton
in Wiltshire (our current El Dorado)) but the proper name is
StourFont or StourHead".   Marnhull gets its name from "Marl
Hill, a hill of marle as the soil is chiefly a white marl or
clay which hardens in air to freestone, easily worked when
first dug but gets hard by time".

The parish church is St Gregory's which you will need to
detour about 1/2 mile to visit.   It has an elegant, lofty
tower of the 15th Century and which is visible for miles in
this pastoral landscape.   Inside, in the North arcade is a
remnant of the 12th Century building in a single carved
capital whilst the 15th Century nave roof and alabaster
figures are particularly fine.

But let's darken proceedings for a few minutes before we go on
our way.   There are several tales of witches around here but
one, which is repeated in a similar vein in many villages in
the West, concerns here a Mrs Fudge who lived in Marnhull
until earlier this century.   She lived in a cottage at the
lower end of Church Hill (not far from St Gregory's) and, as
she stood by her front door one day, she saw a hag-like woman
coming down the hill towards her.   Unfortunately, Mrs Fudge
had the temerity to laugh at the sight of this strange woman
and the hag observed her amusement.   That night, in bed, Mrs
Fudge felt a weight upon her legs which moved slowly up her
body to her chest.   She screamed out in horror and her son
burst into her room.   As soon as the door opened, the heavy
lump fell off and Mrs Fudge distinctly heard the hag walk down
the stairs and out of the door.   Even now, there is an
expression used in this area for anyone who has had a
nightmare.   They are said to have been "hag-ridden".

Anyway, to change the tone (whether for better or worse, I'll
let you decide), we'll move on from tales of witches to tales
of Marnhull ghosts.   At nearby Todber - locally said to be
named from "trod bare" by troops at some great un-named battle
in the area - a great number of human remains were found
during marl quarrying in 1870 and 1871.   Now, at midnight on a
certain date, a funeral was seen crossing Sackmore Lane (the
lane you are in at this moment) from Fillymead to Dunford's.
No mourners attended the ghostly funeral and even the faces of
the bearers were hidden beneath the pall which covered the
coffin.   The same tale is told of Grove Field, near Ash Court
(which once belonged to Catherine Parr, Henry VIII's sixth,
and surviving, wife) which is practically on the same line
from Fillymead to Todber.   Nash Court lies just at the end of
the lane which you will be entering shortly on your way out of
Marnhull.   So, move on now before you get too cold.

At the road junction, turn right and then, immediately opposite the sturdy porch of Banbury House, turn left down Love Lane (Nash Court is down here). Follow this leafy lane, with a few houses tucked away to right and left, to the first bend where you will find a stile made from steel next to a farm gate on the bank facing you. Over the stile, go straight across the field to another stile by the gate opposite. Over this stile, turn sharp left. There is no exit from this field other than through the gates down on your left – at least, not going our way – although the Definitive Map shows an exit near the two Haims Cottages which we will pass later. Aim for the LH corner of this field, basically following the hedge on your left now, to the left of the stile which you have just crossed. In the far corner, go over the farm gate and turn right, aiming towards a house in the dip, with the wire fence leaving you at an angle on your right. At the next gate at the bottom of the field, go out into the road and turn right. About 200 yards down the lane, past Haims Cottages (where our route should have come out of that large field), take the stile in the hedge on your left and go diagonally right to the stile in the RH hedge across the field. This is a particularly wide hedge with the stile tucked away in it, whilst a closer look will reveal that the hedge is built on an embankment. Over this stile, bear left across the corner of the next field.

..turn left down Love Lane – Marnhull – Day 4, This Page

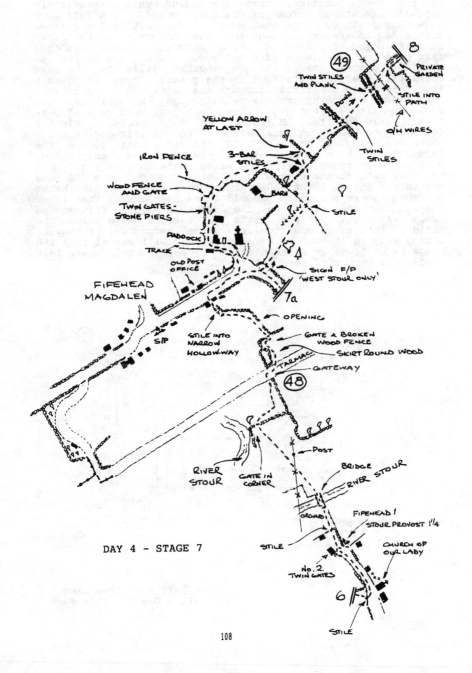

DAY 4 – STAGE 7

DAY 4

STAGE 7 and 7a (First Part)

Marnhull to West Stour

Just cut across the LH corner of this field to the two oaks over by the hedge. Here, a stile leads you out onto the lane opposite the Catholic Church of Our Lady. At this peaceful spot, turn left along the lane, with a wire fence on your left, until you arrive at No 2 on your left. The driveway to No 2 has twin gates but don't shrink from walking straight in - this is the official footpath. The finger post on your right, by the gate post, points to "Fifehead Magdalen 1" whilst the gate on your right leads off to "Stour Provost 1.1/4". Don't go to Stour Provost from here - we want to visit Fifehead Magdalen on the way. Up the drive, go over the stile in the RH corner into an old orchard and cross over the concrete footbridge with the steel handrails. The Stour here has yet to reach the greater volume which we encountered only four miles away (as the crow flies) at Sturminster Newton. The reason for this great reduction in size is that, at Kings Mill Bridge, which is only 3/4 mile upriver from Cut Mill (but which we did not visit due to unsuitable access), the Southward flowing Stour is joined by the Northward flowing River Lydden which, with its tributaries, has been draining the Blackmore Vale. The Lydden, Caundle Brook, the Cam and the Divelish all carry water from the chalk downland watershed which runs East-West across the Southern edge of Blackmore Vale - and all start off by flowing Northwards until becoming the Lydden and joining the River Stour.

However, leave the bridge and follow the faint path to the left of the overhead electric wires support post. Across this long field, aim for the gate in the far LH corner near to a few trees and, through the gate, bear right to follow the hedge in an anti-clockwise direction to the tarmac farm lane which crosses your path at the open end of the field. Turn right on the farm track and through the gateway in the long hedge (probably no gates across the track) and immediately turn left off the track to skirt around the hedged copse on the left. Follow the LH hedge uphill and around the corner to a broken wooden fence and a gateway. Turn left through the opening and into the next field. A hedge will now be on your right. Keep close to it and keep going uphill, past another open hole in the hedge about a quarter of the way along it, until you reach the top RH corner.

As you ascend this field, there are fine distant views across the fields and the flat valley down on your left.

Go over the stile in the corner and into a narrow, dark but short, path which is like a hollow-way and comes out next to the Old School and opposite the Old Post Office. Cross over to the pavement and turn right just before a fine old stone

house along on your left.   There's a telephone box back down
the road if you really can't go on any longer.

However, past a few old stone cottages and a fenced paddock on
your left, you arrive at a   drive   next to the footpath to the
Church of St Mary Magdalene, Fifehead Magdalen.

Of early 14th Century origin,   this   lovely   little church has
been much rebuilt over   the   years but,   notably, not   by the
Victorians.   Its bright   interior   contains a magnificent 18th
Century memorial to Sir   Richard   Newman who died in 1721, his
two wives and three daughters.   Whilst viewing this memorial,
let us not leave without considering the oft used homily about
"swallows" and   "summer".   Outside   this   church,   under the
great yew tree,   on   your   right   as   you   leave the porch, is
interred Thos. Newman who died   in   1688.   Have a look at the
dedication on the side of the stone which faces the church and
read (perhaps wondering which came first):

> Whilst Tower remaine, or spring my yew,
> Here I shall lie as green, young, new,
> ..... news to us good times shall bring,
> One swallow doth not make the spring.

Oh, incidentally, the   "Fifehead" part   of the village's name
comes from its size.   It once   contained   five hides of land -
Fifehide - whilst the   "Magdalen"   derives from the dedication
of its church.

From here, the route to   West   Stour   has   been divided either
side of the church - not by me -   and you now have two choices
for the next 1/2 mile with,   frankly,   little to choose either
way.   For the sake of equality, I will describe both routes.

Firstly, the track to   the   left   of   the church leads through
rather smart gates   to   a   fine   stone house with a lot of
stabling and paddocks so,   if you   don't like horses very much,
go the other way.   However, this   way takes you up the gravel
drive until the track divides   after   the house on your right.
Turn right and   continue,   past   paddocks   on   your   left, to
another pair of   fine iron   gates on   stone piers.   Keep
straight on to a final iron gate, bear diagonally right across
the field   to   the   far RH   corner   and   you   will find   a
three-barred stile with   a   confirmation   yellow   arrow on it.
Here is where the alternatives meet.

Secondly, past the iron gates   in   the   stone wall in the road
after the church and the   RH bend   in   the   road, go over the
stile in the hedge on   the   left.   This   is   the way to "West
Stour" but do as the notice   says   and "Keep to the footpath",
past the dead oak with the yellow arrow nailed to its LH side.
Keeping the iron fence,   a   fine   cedar   and an embankment, in
that order, on your left,   you   come   to   a stile in the wire
fence across your path.   In   the   next   field, aim diagonally
left towards a three-barred   stile   in the hedge on your left.

Climb over (it has no foot plank) and bear right to the next three-barred stile. Here, you meet up with the first alternative.

Now bear with me - there is another route to West Stour which takes us via the delightful village of Stour Provost (my own preference, I must admit). If you would like to come with me to enjoy its lovely cottages, its fine church and mill, together with a stroll along the edge of the Stour, go back to the road and turn downhill, past the stile to "West Stour - Keep to the Footpath" and keep on down the road until you arrive at the next stile, about 100 yards further on. You will find all of this on Stage 7a details.

However, if you can easily resist any more villages (as lovely as they may prove), climb over this three-barred stile and keep to the RH hedge straight through the next field, to a pair of stiles in the wide hedge ahead of you. You now emerge at the top of a steeply sloping field which you go straight down to another pair of stiles with a plank bridge across a ditch. Coming out into the next field, cross over and, keeping to the left side of the gantry supporting overhead wires, go over the stile in the hedge facing you. Don't miss the stile and go wandering up the wider part of the field to the left of it as this will bring you to private farm buildings and a dead end. Over the stile, an unkempt hedge on your left and a low, wooden garden fence (more of a single rail, really) lead you past a private garden.

"One swallow doth not make the spring"
Fifehead Magdalen - Day 4, Page 110

111

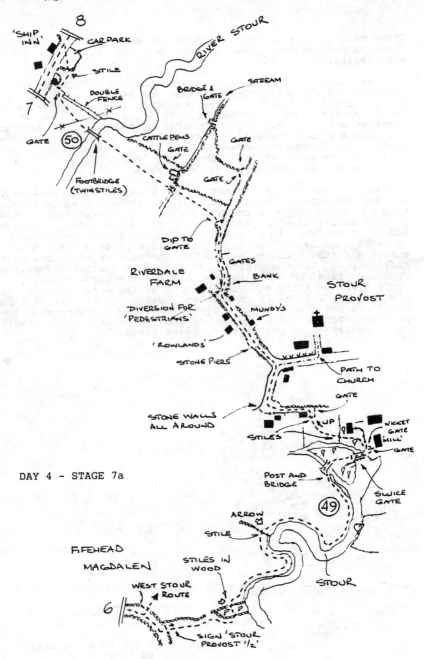

WEST STOUR

8

'SHIP INN'

CAR PARK

STILE

DOUBLE FENCE

7

GATE

50

RIVER STOUR

STREAM

BRIDGE & GATE

CATTLE PENS

GATE

GATE

GATE

GATE

FOOTBRIDGE (TWIN STILES)

DIP TO GATE

RIVERDALE FARM

GATES

BANK

STOUR PROVOST

DIVERSION FOR 'PEDESTRIANS'

MUNDY'S

'ROWLANDS'

STONE PIERS

PATH TO CHURCH

GATE

STONE WALLS ALL AROUND

STILES

UP

WICKET GATE

MILL

GATE

DAY 4 - STAGE 7a

POST AND BRIDGE

49

SLUICE GATE

ARROW

STILE

FIFEHEAD MAGDALEN

STILES IN WOOD

WEST STOUR ROUTE

6

STOUR

SIGN 'STOUR PROVOST ½'

DAY 4

STAGE 7a (Second Part)

Fifehead Magdalen to West Stour via Stour Provost

After passing the stile for "West Stour", continue down the lane for another 100 yards and take the next farm gate in the hedge on your left which is signposted "Footpath Stour Provost 1/2". Keep to the LH hedge as the field drops down towards the River. Ignore an opening in the hedge and keep on down almost to the River edge. Here, go over the stile on your left into a very small wood and out the other side over a second stile. A yellow arrow guides you sharp right to a wire fence along the edge of the Stour. Follow the River upstream to a short section of wooden fence and a stile. Cross over the stile and keep following the "oxbow" of the River - no fence on our side now - all the way to the next footbridge, a good 250 yards riverside stroll. On the way, there are lovely views of the sluice gates, pool and mill complex on the other side. Squeeze around the arrowed post by the gate and the "Private Fishing" sign and cross the bridge.

On the other side, the island between two branches of the Stour has been planted with specimen trees and the grass is well mowed. Turn right and go through the next gate onto the bridge over the sluice gates. This is a lovely spot, through private land, so tread quietly. Before going through the next farm gate, have a look at the plaque on the mill wall in this field. Then, through the gate, turn through the wicket gate on your immediate left to bring you out on the other side of the second tributary. Cross the "garden" lawn to a stile in the wire fence past the specimen trees and go over the stile into the field which slopes steeply up to your right. Head diagonally up this field to the top by a low stone barn. Here, go over the stile by the gate and walk along the wide, grassy track to a selection of stone garden walls of varying heights on left and right. Bearing right, the track becomes a tarmac surface with grass up the middle and soon emerges, between the high stone wall on your left and a hedged garden on your right, onto a T-junction. We will be going left here to West Stour but, firstly, take a stroll into Stour Provost and have a look at the stone cottages, the Church of St Michael which is up the grassy path just before the first street-aligned cottage on your left, and maybe the inn which is a few steps around the next right hand corner.

Stour Provost is named after a derivation of Preaux or Priaulx, the monastery to which this land belonged in ancient times. Preaux is in a valley on the River Rille near Pont Audemer in France.

The Church of St Michael was restored in 1838 but retains its early 14th and 15th Century character and is well worth a visit. It has a fine, big lych gate and an avenue of pollarded trees to the main porch. It has a lovely chancel ceiling whilst, on the South side, it has some elegant lancet windows with four Early-English columns and also a "striking clock with no face" which was built by William Monk of Berwick St John in 1735.

Back to the lane where we entered Stour Provost, carry on down the steep sided, shady gulley past several attractive stone cottages and the really pretty garden of "Rowlands" on your left. A little further down the lane, at Riversdale Farm, take the signed "Pedestrians" diversion around the right of the farmyard. A rebuilt track, cut into the slopes on your right, takes you on into a hedged farm track. Take the first gate, down an angled dip on your left, into the large field. Aim for the far, low down, RH corner of the field at the bottom end of the long hedge which faced you when you came through the gate. In that corner, you will find a gateway bridging a small stream which leads you into the next very large field. Keep following the same direction with a hedge about 20 yards to your right. This leads to a solid wooden footbridge (which you can see from the other side of this field if you look hard enough), with stiles at either end, across the Stour. A very pleasant spot with water lilies in the summer.

Now continue up the steeply sloping field, approximately NNW, coming closer to the double wire fence on your right as you climb upwards. At the top of the field, keep to the wire fence and go through the farm gate just before the cottage at the top. In the next small field, cross over a space of just 30 yards to a stile in the wooden fence which borders the car park of the Ship Inn, West Stour.

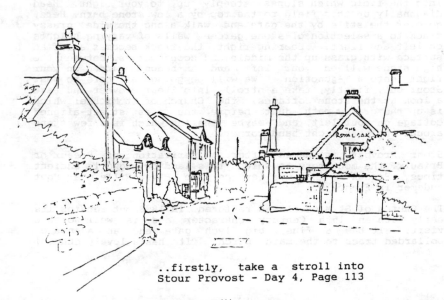

..firstly, take a stroll into
Stour Provost - Day 4, Page 113

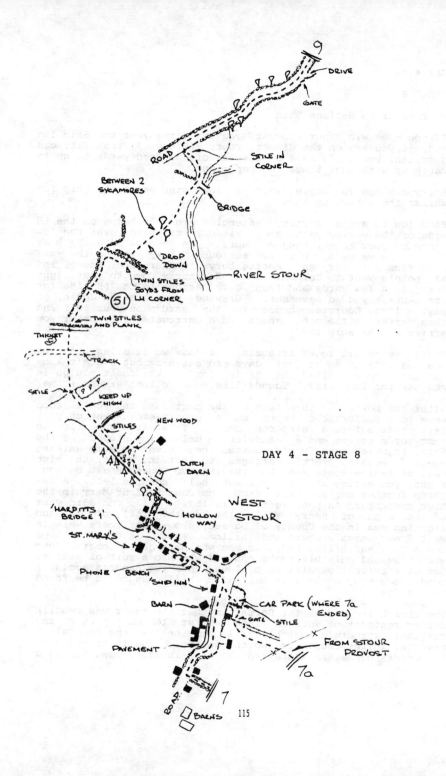

DRIVE

GATE

ROAD

STILE IN CORNER

BETWEEN 2 SYCAMORES

BRIDGE

DROP DOWN

RIVER STOUR

TWIN STILES 50YDS FROM LH CORNER

(51)

TWIN STILES AND PLANK

THICKET

TRACK

STILE

KEEP UP HIGH

STILES

NEW WOOD

DUTCH BARN

DAY 4 - STAGE 8

WEST STOUR

'HARPITTS BRIDGE'

HOLLOW WAY

ST. MARY'S

PHONE   BENCH

'SHIP INN'

BARN

CAR PARK (WHERE 7a ENDED)

GATE   STILE

PAVEMENT

FROM STOUR PROVOST

7a

ROAD   7

BARNS   115

DAY 4

STAGE 8

West Stour to Nations Road

If you came via Stour Provost, you are already at the Ship Inn but, if you are on the direct route (Stage 7) from Fifehead Magdalen, you still have a couple of hundred yards to go to catch up with your Stage 7a companions.

So, you Stage 7a people wait a few minutes at the Ship Inn whilst the others do this:

Bend low to avoid getting entangled in the hedge on the LH side of the narrow path and, without tripping over the low fence on your right, keep on until you emerge onto the busy A30. Be warned! This is seriously busy, being the main road from Salisbury and Shaftesbury to Sherborne, Yeovil and all points West to Cornwalll. So hurry down to your right for just a few yards and then dive across to the LH side for the sanctuary of a pavement. Drawing deep breaths again, go past a large Georgian house in the garden on your left and then, after cattle pens, sheds and a corrugated iron barn, you arrive at the Ship Inn.

Right, we're all together again. I know we're miles from the sea and it's taken us four days to get here but I don't know why this inn is called the "Ship Inn". Why don't you go in and ask the landlord? Sounds like an excellent excuse to me.

After the hostelry, turn left up the next lane and you'll soon come to a comfortable bench on a grassy embankment on your left, just before a telephone box. This is a good spot to rest for a coffee and a sandwich - unless you stopped at the Ship, in which case you'd better get down to some walking again. Passing pretty cottages to left and right, the high wall of Ashley House and the turning to Church House on your right, you arrive at the village hall on the left. A few yards further on, you will find the Church of St Mary in the high churchyard on your left. In 1541 - 1542, the 33rd year of the reign of Henry VIII, the muster roll of fit and fighting men in the County of Dorset, shows that there were in West Stour seven archers and billmen (that is they had bows and arrows and billhooks), two men who were just archers, four who possessed only billhooks and one who had a suit of armour. Out of a current population of less than two hundred souls, I wonder how many archers or men with billhooks could be found here today.

The church is unusual for Dorset in that the tower was rebuilt during restoration work in 1840 whilst the only part of the original structure which still remains is the chancel. A memorial in the chapel is worth noting. The inscription to the memory of Martin Meateyard who died in 1733, aged 63, is a salutary reminder of why we're out enjoying this wonderful fresh air so much:

> Behold all you that here pass by
> This house of clay wherein I ly.
> Your mortal state behold and see
> For as I am so must you be.

Now, opposite the church on the LH bend in the lane, turn down the path, signed "Harpitts Bridge 1", and descend into a shady hollow-way which we follow to a wooden fence at the other end. Over the fence, join a tarmac drive coming from your right and turn left onto it but, before the track bends right again, turn off into a new wood and go over the stile in the LH corner into a field which slopes away to your right into the River valley. Keep close to the wooden fence and the firs on your left and go over the next stile by the gate ahead of you into yet another field. Keep up high in this field and aim past the LH end of the new wood (wire fenced in) which is facing you. Here you will find a stile in the wire fence (not into the wood) into a very large field which drops away ahead of you and also slopes down into the valley on your right. The next stile is not easy to find but, if you keep straight across the field, keeping a thicket within the field about 50 yards to the left of you, you will find a twin stile and a single plank over the ditch in the thick hedge at the bottom of the field. In the next field, there is a hedge on your left which you follow to the gate in the LH corner ahead of you.

Take care in this field. The way out is even more difficult to find (unless the facing hedge has been cut since I struggled through). Keep to the LH hedge until you get to the gate in the LH corner of the field. Do not go through the gate but turn right and follow the hedge for 50 yards downhill, searching in the thick hedge on your left all the time. Here, you will find another pair of stiles on the other side of which the field slopes away to the River at its foot.

Take the line between the two sycamores ahead of you, diagonally downhill to your right, towards the River and a distant footbridge. Go past the bridge and through the gap in the corner of your field into a smaller area in which cows are known to congregate. Turn left, away from the River and alongside the wire fence, to a stile onto the road and turn right. Sadly, due to the lack of footpaths or any suitable alternatives, we now have about a mile of road walking to do but it's quite steady and it's less than two miles altogether to the end of today's excursion. Just follow the road between high hedges and fine old trees to a fenced drive to "Wool House" on your right.

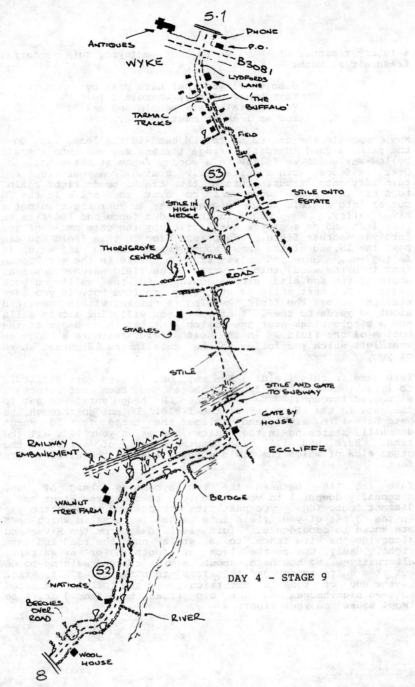

5.1

PHONE

ANTIQUES

P.O.

WYKE

B3081

LYDFORDS LANE

'THE BUFFALO'

TARMAC TRACKS

FIELD

53

STILE

STILE ONTO ESTATE

STILE IN HIGH HEDGE

THORNGROVE CENTRE

STILE

ROAD

STABLES

STILE

STILE AND GATE TO SUBWAY

GATE BY HOUSE

RAILWAY EMBANKMENT

ECCLIFFE

BRIDGE

WALNUT TREE FARM

52

'NATIONS'

DAY 4 - STAGE 9

BEECHES OVER ROAD

RIVER

8

WOOL HOUSE

DAY 4

STAGE 9

Nations Road to Wyke

Passing Wool House and the lane off to your left, go under
some large beech trees which overhang the road from left to
right and keep going, with the Stour sunken in the fields on
your right, not far below road level. Past "Nations" and
"Walnut Tree Farm" on the left, the road bends left and goes
under the railway embankment but turn off right here and keep
on as a small stream runs under the road to join the Stour on
your right. The signpost points to "Eccliffe" and, in a few
yards, we meet the Stour again as it runs under a farm bridge
just off the road on the right.

All along here, we are following the railway line behind the
hedge on your left and, when the lane turns to the right by a
cottage, turn left and go through a farm gate next to the
cottage and into a field which is between the lane and the
embankment. Aim directly at the railway line and you will
find an opening in the wooden fence on your right. Go right
through the opening and bear left towards a stile in the fence
parallel to the embankment (mind the grating over a well or
drain en route). Over the stile, enter the tunnel which
leads you under the railway line and out into the field on the
other side.

Cross the field and go over the stile in the wire fence into
the next field. Here, follow the line of the hedge on your
right to a stile in the RH corner and go over into the next
field before the road. Over the last stile onto the road,
cross over and go up the driveway opposite, to the left of the
house, signed for "Thorngrove Centre". Up the wide driveway,
look for the stile over the wire fence on your right which you
climb over into the next field. Cross this field to another
stile in the high, tree-filled hedge opposite. This leads you
into an open field, beyond which are the outermost dwellings
of Wyke and Gillingham. Aim to the right of the overhead
cable post.

From this field can be made out a highly significant landmark
- for this Walk, at least. Away in the distance, you can see
the bulk of Alfred's Tower which stands close to the head of
the valley in which the Stour rises - Journey's end at
Stourhead and Six Wells Bottom.

For now, however, as the path clearly goes to a stile which
leads into the estate of houses, bear off and go over a stile
in the hedge on your left. In this next large field follow
the line of fences and houses on your right until you arrive
in the distant RH corner and yet another stile - the last
today. Over the stile, between a wooden fence on the left
and a hedge on the right, behind both of which are now several

houses, follow the path - now a tarmac lane - all the way to join the B3081. On the way, you will notice "The Buffalo" on your right - and, no, I don't know why it should be called "The Buffalo" - perhaps you should go in and ask. But we've used that excuse already today, so perhaps not. Anyway, at the end of the lane, we find that it is called Lydford Lane and the road opposite, Pound Lane, leads us onto Day 5 and the Grand Finale.

For now, there is plenty of accommodation to be found in Wyke or Gillingham just down the road on the right - and there are plenty of buses as well. So I'll leave you here until Day 5.

Actually, if you go into Gillingham, the small river which you cross over firstly on the way in is the Stour. The wider river which runs through the other end of town is Shreen Water, although the two will meet to the South of the High Street in Gillingham.

Now we don't have much information about Wyke except from Rev Hutchins who informs us that it is a "Hamlet 1/2 mile NW from Gillingham" and that it is "named after Richard de Wyke 2 Ed III".

Gillingham, on the other hand, sported a Palace which was built by King John in 1199 as a hunting residence, the ramparts and foundations of which still exist 1/2 mile East outside the town at Kings Court. The Church of the Blessed Virgin, St Mary was, more typically for Dorset, restored in 1838-39 whilst the chancel is 14th Century and is five bays long. The tower is blessed with typical Somerset tracery - a sure sign that we are only 2.1/2 miles from the County boundary.

By the way, all of the mileages from here on will assume that everybody went via Stour Provost to West Stour and did the extra mile - so total mileage from here to the end of our journey will be starting at 53.1/2 miles from the beginning of Day 5.

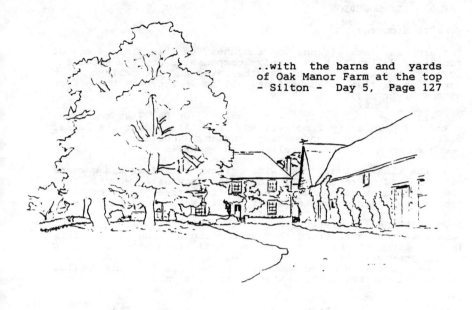

..with the barns and yards
of Oak Manor Farm at the top
- Silton - Day 5, Page 127

..a beautiful square, stone summer
house - Stourhead - Day 5, Page 137

DAY 5 - INTRODUCTION

Wyke to Stourton

The singular lack of inns and churches on this final stage of
the Stour Valley Path is amply compensated by the beautiful
scenery, the woods, the hills, the lakes and the valleys which
have been waiting to enchant us all as we approach the source
of the River Stour.

Whereas we enjoyed almost level walking on Day 4 as the River
meandered carelessly from village to village over the Dorset
plains, we are now approaching ancient woodland, huge oaks,
beeches and chestnuts in valleys and on hills.

From the final height, the wide grassy ride from the gardens
of Stourhead up to the hill fort at Park Hill, we will take
the final faint path down through the trees and bracken to
find three lakes strung together in Six Wells Bottom.

Beyond is the dry valley floor - the lakes are fed by springs
(and have been ever since they were medieval fish ponds). This
is the source of the River Stour and, from here, this pure
clean water will flow past all of the villages, mills and
bridges which we visited on our journey, to join the English
Channel at Christchurch. What a fabulous walk!

	STAGE	MILES	TOTAL
1	Wyke to Pierston Fields	1.50	1.50
2	Pierston Fields to Stocking Bridge	1	2.50
3	Stocking Bridge to Pen Mill	1.50	4
4	Pen Mill to Bonham	.75	4.75
5	Bonham to Six Wells Bottom	.75	5.50
6	Six Wells Bottom to Stourton	1.50	7

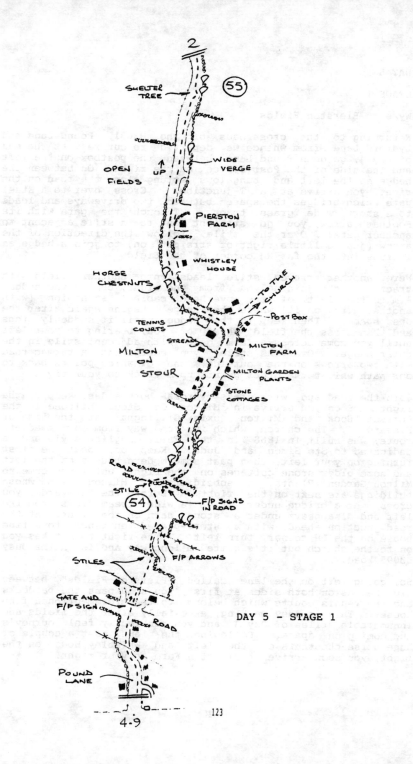

DAY 5 - STAGE 1

123

DAY 5

STAGE 1

Wyke to Pierston Fields

Returning to the crossroads of the B3081, Pound Lane and Lydford Lane, from whence we departed to our rest at the end of Day 4, go down Pound Lane between the postbox on the left and the side of the Post Office on the right. On between the hedge on the left and bungalows strung along the road on the right, you arrive at a T-junction. Cross over to a steel gate which bridges the space between two driveways and leads to a short, wide grass track. Through the gate with its Footpath arrow, you go straight on to a stile adjacent to another gate. Over the stile, follow the direction of the arrow (just a little right of straight on) to join a hedge as it runs into the far RH corner of the field.

Here, another arrowed stile leads into another field with tractor tracks joining you from the right, behind the hedge. Aim to the left of the overhead cables' stanchion (with another arrow on it) where the hedge begins again after the open space. Then keep to the hedge until it suddenly stops and then cross the field ahead of you, bearing to your left until you come across a farm gate with adjacent stile in the outer hedge. Over the stile, you emerge onto a tarmac road with two arrows on the outside, one of which points back to our path whilst the other points up a track to your right.

Join the road and, with grass verges both sides, keep to the right. Soon you arrive in Milton On Stour, Miltone in the Domesday Book and Milton juxta Gillingham at the time of Richard II. The church, which is some way from our immediate route, was built in 1868 in the Early English style and is dedicated to Sts Simon and Jude. Keep on, past the first turning on your left, then past some modern houses on the left and some older stone cottages on the right, until you come to Milton Garden Plants, a subsidiary of Milton Farm whose buildings are next on the right. Before the farmyards, you cross over a bridge under which a wide stream flows from the left and disappears under a stone barn on the right. At the road junction ahead, with a stone-piered entrance to a fine house on the LH corner, turn left. The right turn takes you on to the church but it's quite a long way and is on the busy B3095 road.

So, going left on the lane called "Pierston Fields", between high hedges on both sides at first, you soon pass the paddocks and the tennis courts which belong to the aforementioned fine house. This is easy walking, especially after the fields and innumerable stiles of Day 4, and you can really feel journey's end coming on apace. Following the lane, past a couple of huge horse-chestnuts on the left and Whistley House on the right, you soon arrive at Pierston Farm on your right.

Pierston formerly shared a tithing with Milton On Stour and consisted of "a manor, a hamlet and a farm" and, according to Hutchins, "The River Stour abounds with trout, running through the centre of the premises".

Now there is a wide verge on the right as you ascend slightly with open fields on your left and hedged fields on your right. Reaching the top of the rise, there are still open fields on the left whilst rows of old trees show where the lines of the streams run in the valley bottoms on either side. The one on the right carries the Stour. As you descend again, as the verge has disappeared from your right and been replaced by a ditch, a bank and a wire fence, you will see a farm gate and a big, old oak perched atop the bank on your right. I have reason to be grateful to this tree - it sheltered me from a sudden, fierce downpour which had crept up on me from behind.

It was at this point, on the last Day, that I suddenly thought of a good reason for not walking from sea to source - the sun might very well be shining from behind as you walk from South to North, but changes of weather usually arrive from the South-West as well and you can't see the clouds building up.

..the Church of St Nicholas appears.. above a long, stone wall - Silton - Day 5, Page 127

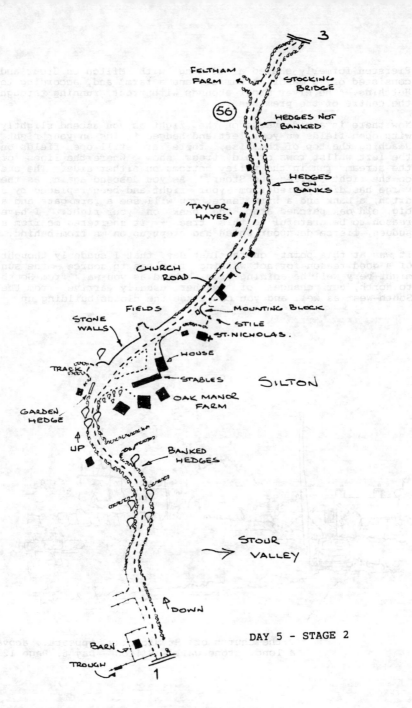

3

FELTHAM
FARM

STOCKING
BRIDGE

(56)

HEDGES NOT
BANKED

HEDGES
ON
BANKS

'TAYLOR
HAYES'

CHURCH
ROAD

FIELDS

MOUNTING BLOCK

STILE

STONE
WALLS

ST. NICHOLAS.

SILTON

HOUSE

TRACK

STABLES

GARDEN
HEDGE

OAK MANOR
FARM

UP

BANKED
HEDGES

STOUR
VALLEY

DOWN

DAY 5 – STAGE 2

BARN

TROUGH

1

DAY 5

STAGE 2

Pierston Fields to Stocking Bridge

Down the lane, you pass an open barn on the left and then a turning left to "Whistley Farm and Whistley Water". Carry on up the hedged and banked lane, now with overhanging trees, to the top of the rise. You are now arriving in the hamlet of Silton with the barns and yards of Oak Manor Farm at the top on your right. The area around the farmhouse and its stables has been beautifully landscaped with new trees and trimmed grass open areas on the right and there remains a really old, gnarled tree right by the side of the road. Over the stone field wall on the left, there are some fine farmland views.

Continuing down the lane, the Church of St Nicholas appears over on the right above a long, stone wall and, within a few more paces, the Church entrance is found next to a mounting block and a stile on the right which we do not want on this occasion.

Before leaving the Church, you may like to go inside to have a look at the roof's open timbers of massive oak and the beautiful fan-traceried roof of the vestry.

Rev Hutchins describes the fine setting of St Nicholas' Church thus: "It stands on a knoll in the midst of a rich and well-wooded country; and the views from the churchyard are peculiarly pleasing". We must surely agree with this observation. Apart from the features which have already been mentioned, the Church was "much improved" in 1860 although some of its original 13th Century sections still remain.

Just a little further down the lane, stone piers and iron gates on your right lead to a large, stone house with a lovely garden and, continuing along Church Road, you pass "Taylor Hayes" cottages on the left and a continuous high hedge on the right. After the banked hedges have run out, at least they have descended from their banks, a lane turns off left to "Feltham Farm Only". Keep straight on past this turning and, where the road goes over a small stream or ditch, just keep on going - this is Stocking Bridge.

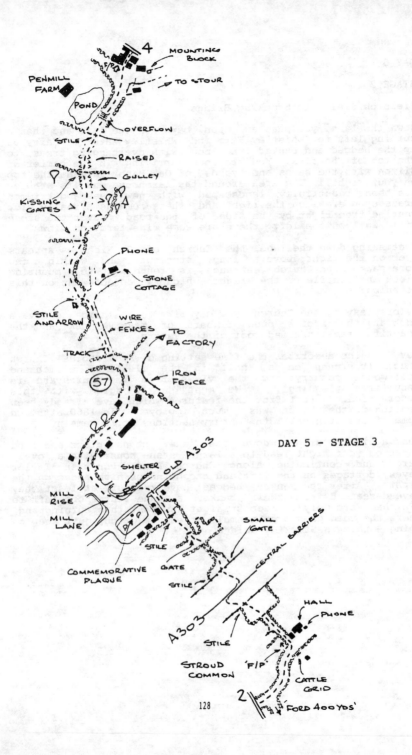

4 MOUNTING BLOCK

F/P

TO STOUR

PENMILL FARM

POND

OVERFLOW

STILE

RAISED

GULLEY

KISSING GATES

PHONE

STONE COTTAGE

STILE AND ARROW

WIRE FENCES

TO FACTORY

TRACK

57

IRON FENCE

ROAD

DAY 5 - STAGE 3

SHELTER

OLD A303

MILL RISE

MILL LANE

STILE

SMALL GATE

GATE

COMMEMORATIVE PLAQUE

STILE

CENTRAL BARRIERS

HALL

PHONE

A303

STILE

STROUD COMMON

'F/P'

CATTLE GRID

2

FORD 400 YDS'

DAY 5

STAGE 3

Stocking Bridge to Pen Mill

After the bridge, keep on past the "Ford 400 yards" turning on
the right, until a right bend brings you to a house, the
village hall and a telephone box on your left, just opposite a
cattle grid in the entrance to a house on your right. Turn
left, just before the house on the left, onto a track which
carries a footpath sign to "Bourton 1/2". On your left up
this track is Stroud Common which, before the Enclosure Acts,
provided free grazing for a few tenants who lived close by.
There is still a "Stroud Paddock" on your left. At the end
of the track, go around the gate and cross the small field,
aiming for the LH corner where the hedge on your left meets a
wooden fence across your path.

Go over the stile and down the paved steps in the embankment
to the busy A303 - Bourton By-Pass - at the bottom. Take
great care - this is alien territory to pedestrians!

Safely negotiating the safety barrier in the central
reservation, cross to the steps back up the opposite
embankment to a stile at the top. Over the stile, you will
find a small gate on your right and another stile on your
left. Ignore them both and plough down the hedged pathway
which is directly facing you until you emerge at a junction of
farm gates with a wide track from East View Farm on your left.

Go over the gate into the field which is almost opposite you
and follow the RH hedge down to the stile in the wire fence at
the bottom, with some houses on your left and the hedge on
your right as you continue along the pathway to the old A303
through Bourton. There is a Petrol Station just down the
road to your right if you need any provisions. Anyway, cross
over to the pavement opposite and turn left, passing a bus
shelter on your way to the next road on the right, which is
Mill Lane. On the reservation opposite the bus shelter is a
huge rock with a commemorative plaque which was erected by the
much-relieved Celebration Committee of Bourton when the
By-Pass finally saved them and neighbouring Zeals from the
thundering traffic.

Turn up Mill Lane and, passing New Close on the right and Mill
Rise on the left, continue down the old, hedged lane, passing
houses high up on your right, until you arrive at a T-junction
with an iron fence opposite. Here, turn sharp left and
follow the hedge around the hairpin. Do not go down to
Bourton Mill or through the first gate which is facing you.
Go instead through the second gate which leads you onto an
uphill track between wire fences. This track overlooks the
Mill Factory down on your right. Bourton Mill once employed
200 people in a foundry and in the manufacture of sacks. It

was powered by a huge 60ft diameter water wheel - one of the biggest in the Country.

With a hedge joining you from your left, continue to where the lane bears right towards a stone cottage and a telephone box facing you. An arrow directs you over the next stile by a gate to the left of all this and you now follow the hedge on your right to the next gate. Here, the field rises quite steeply on your left and drops away on your right (to the Stour valley). Through the next gate, follow the grassy track across the next field with a hedge and trees having gone off down into the valley. Down a short, grassy gulley you come to a kissing gate next to a farm gate in the hedge. Through here, keep to the raised path with marshy ground on either side as it drops down to a gate and stile in the hedge and fence at the bottom. The lovely white and stone house in the grounds with the pond is Penmill Farm. Passing alongside the pond, and over the concrete outflow from the pond into the steep valley on your right, follow the path to its junction with a tarmac road.

The road past the mounting block on your right leads down to the River but you need to cross over and go between the barn and garage, signposted "Coombe Street 1/2" and "Pear Ash 3/4".

Turn left, just before the house on the left - Stroud Common - Day 5, Page 129

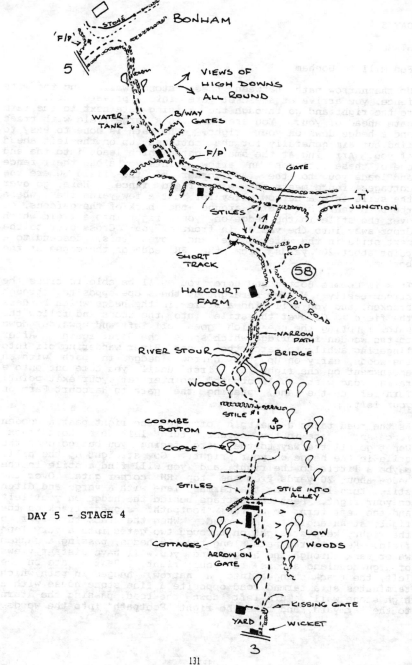

BONHAM

STONE

'F/P'

5

VIEWS OF
HIGH DOWNS
ALL ROUND

WATER
TANK

B/WAY
GATES

'F/P'

GATE

'T'
JUNCTION

STILES

UP

SHORT
TRACK

ROAD

58

HARCOURT
FARM

'B/D' ROAD

NARROW
PATH

RIVER STOUR

BRIDGE

WOODS

STILE

UP

COOMBE
BOTTOM

COPSE

STILES

STILE INTO
ALLEY

DAY 5 - STAGE 4

LOW
WOODS

COTTAGES

ARROW ON
GATE

KISSING GATE

YARD

WICKET

3

DAY 5

STAGE 4

Pen Mill to Bonham

Up the narrow path between these stone walls and the wire
fence, you arrive at a wicket gate into a private yard. Keep
to the right and go through the kissing gate next to the farm
gate ahead of you. You are now in a large field with trees
and a hedge down on your right. The path is none to easy to
find but aim generally for the cottages up on the left ahead
of you. Arriving at the small gate which leads into the end
one of these cottages, an arrow points you along their fence
and leads you to the far corner of the field where the
cottages' fence meets the wire field fence. Here, go over
the stile into a narrow alley for just a few yards then, where
the path veers off left around the back of the gardens, go
over the stile in the hedge on your right into a field which
drops away into the valley in front of you. Cross over to the
next stile in the wire fence and, over this, descend to a
point about 20 yards from the RH end of the copse at the
bottom.

This is Coombe Bottom and here you will be able to cross the
stream easily. Now go straight up the slope opposite, through
bracken, and you will find a stile in the hedge which borders
the field. Go over the stile into the woods and follow the
path, ignoring the one which goes off left and upwards, down
to the wooden footbridge which spans the Stour again. After
lingering awhile to watch the young River wandering off into
the woods, carry on up the narrow, hedged-in path with an
embankment on the right at first until you come out onto a
tarmac road with a "Footpath" pointer at your exit point.
Turn left up the lane, passing the gate to Harcourt Farm on
your left.

As the road takes a hairpin off to the right past a wooden
fence and a gate in the corner, turn left up a short track.
Don't go all the way to the gate facing you but go over the
stile in the hedge on your right. Go straight up the hill,
maybe a little to the right, and you will find a stile in the
hedge about 20 yards from the top RH corner gate. Over the
stile, turn left along the tarmac lane with a verge and ditch
on your right. Past the cottage behind the hedge on your left
and the left turn, go up the "Footpath" signed track on the
right, at an angle to the road. When the track turns off to
the right, keep straight on through two gates into a very long
field. Keep to the path along the LH hedge, passing a sunken
water tank through the hedge, and you will have distant views
of high downland across to your right. Past a gate on the
left, the track changes into a narrow, hedged-in path which
terminates at a tarmac road opposite a fine stone house with a
high stone wall. Turn left down the road, passing the turn
to the farmyard, and take the right "Footpath" into the woods.

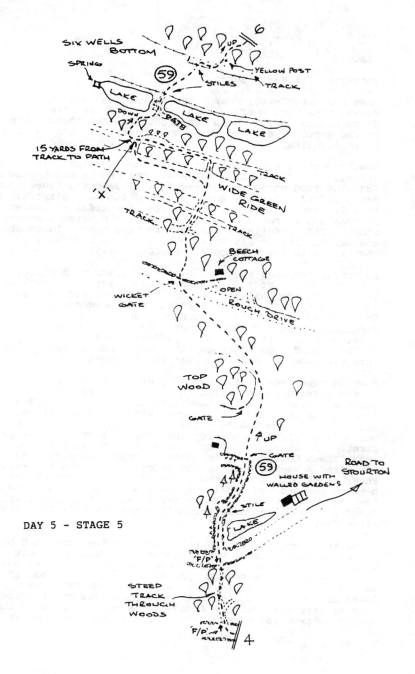

SIX WELLS BOTTOM

SPRING

59

LAKE

YELLOW POST

STILES

TRACK

DOWN

LAKE PATH

LAKE

LAKE

15 YARDS FROM TRACK TO PATH

TRACK

'X'

WIDE GREEN RIDE

TRACK

TRACK

BEECH COTTAGE

WICKET GATE

OPEN

ROUGH DRIVE

TOP WOOD

GATE

UP

GATE

59

HOUSE WITH WALLED GARDENS

ROAD TO STOURTON

STILE

LAKE

DAY 5 - STAGE 5

'F/P'

STEEP TRACK THROUGH WOODS

'F/P'

4

DAY 5

STAGE 5

Bonham to Six Wells Bottom

Down the steep path, used by horses as was the lane into
Bonham, the path veers off to the right for "Permit-holding
Horse Riders Only". Keep straight on down through the trees
to the bottom where you come out onto the lane, with a good
track opposite.

Now, for those who would like to go straight into Stourton
village, for Stourhead Gardens, Tea Rooms and Spread Eagle
Inn, the road going to the right will lead you there. In the
National Trust Gardens you will find two of the springs which
feed Stourhead lake - these are beautifully staged with
statues and a grotto but they are not the prime source of the
Stour. This privilege belongs to the higher lakes which we
are off to find at Six Wells Bottom - and we will be coming
back round to the village afterwards, anyway.

So, cross the road and head up the track with a field and a
lake on your right and a drop down from the track on your
left. Up the valley, beyond the lake, you can see an old
cottage with its walled gardens and paddocks still intact.
Uphill now, with a short coppiced hedge and a stile on your
right, past the "Private Woods, No Dogs" sign and some lofty
pines on your left, the road suddenly bears off to the left.
At this bend, go through the gate which keeps you in a
straight line and into the open field beyond.

Down on your right, you now get your first glimpse of the edge
of Stourhead Gardens whilst thick woods carpet the valley and
hills opposite. In the Domesday Book, Stourton had a forest
"one league long and one league wide". Ahead of you, up to
your left is "Top Wood". Aim for the far RH end of the fence
surrounding it, keeping to the upper slopes of the park at
first. Reaching the woods, head for the junction of tracks
near "Beech Cottage" (the only cottage in sight) where you
will find a wicket gate in the hedge. Through the gate, you
enter thick pine and hardwood forests which carpet the ridge
between you and your goal but, before you go through the gate,
look left and you will see Alfred's Tower which you spotted on
Day 4 as you walked near Marnhull - but now it's less than two
miles away.

Go up the steep and narrow path through the trees and bracken
to join a forest track which comes in from your left. Keep
straight on upwards, crossing another track before emerging
onto an amazingly wide and grassy ride which leads from the
Gardens to Park Hill fort. It's all downhill now to the
lakes at Six Wells Bottom but, be warned, the final descending
path is very difficult to find - it's not as clear as the one
coming up from the gate. So, cross over the ride and keep

straight on, down an equally grassy track and turn left onto the track at the other end - or turn left up the grassy ride and take the next track down on your right. Either way, you need to end up at the junction of the second track from the top ride with the parallel track on the downward side - marked with a "X" on the sketch map.

Now pace out 15 yards along the long track and go into the trees on your right. Here, you will find an obvious, but little used, path down through the trees and bracken - steep in parts and with dirt steps nearer the bottom.

Emerging at its end, you come onto a path which comes from the Gardens on your right. Join this path as it turns, between two of the source lakes, to a stile in a wire fence. Over the fence, you are in Six Wells Bottom.

The hills on either side and up the valley on your left all drain into this valley although, beyond the first lake, the valley is dry. Rain water percolates down through the soil and comes into these lakes through springs. Formerly, before these were medieval fish ponds, the springs would have been visible in the valley floor as are several remaining springs which are scattered among the encircling wooded slopes and higher up the valley. (Diligent search would eventually uncover these springs but the water seeps back into the soil to emerge into the lower lakes anyway).

These lakes are the source of our River Stour. You have arrived!

Savour the moment and consider how all of the water which starts here will eventually pass through the lakes, under the bridges, through the mills, around the villages, into the towns, over the ford which you waded across all that time ago, and out into the English Channel in 59 miles from here.

To celebrate this occasion, let's go on to Stourton for a cup of tea in the Village Hall Tea Rooms, a pint in the Spread Eagle Inn or, maybe, a little contemplation in St Peter's Church. A stroll around Stourhead Gardens would be lovely as well to view the Grotto's springs - after all, it's only been a short walk today.

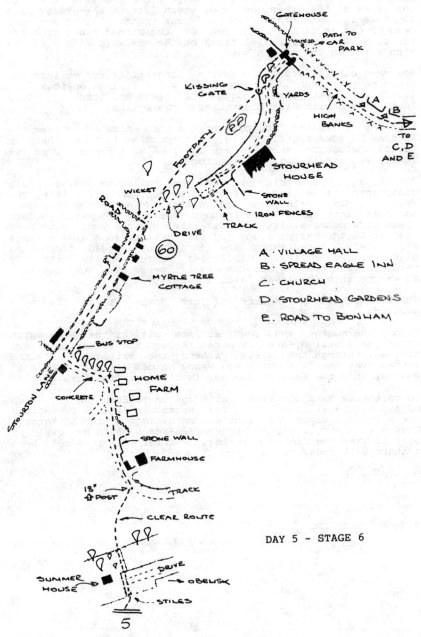

GATEHOUSE

PATH TO
CAR
PARK

KISSING
GATE

YARDS

A

B

HIGH
BANKS

TO
C, D
AND E

FOOTPATH

STOURHEAD
HOUSE

WICKET

STONE
WALL

ROAD

IRON FENCES

DRIVE

TRACK

60

A · VILLAGE HALL
B · SPREAD EAGLE INN
C · CHURCH
D · STOURHEAD GARDENS
E · ROAD TO BONHAM

MYRTLE TREE
COTTAGE

BUS STOP

HOME
FARM

STOURTON LANE

CONCRETE

STONE WALL

FARMHOUSE

18"
POST

TRACK

CLEAR ROUTE

DAY 5 - STAGE 6

DRIVE

SUMMER
HOUSE

OBELISK

STILES

5

136

DAY 5

STAGE 6

Six Wells Bottom to Stourton

Exhilerated and regretful at the same time, leave Six Wells
Bottom by continuing across the valley floor and up to the
stile in the wire fence opposite. Over the stile, turn right
on the track, but only for a few steps. In about 30 yards,
scour the wooded slopes on your left for a small yellow post
sticking up out of the bracken and head up the faint path
towards it. Past it, the path becomes clearer and steeper
until you come to a stile in the fence at the top.

Over the fence, an unexpected scene greets you. There are
smartly mowed lawns, a neat gravel driveway and a beautiful
square, stone summer house all awaiting your arrival. Over
the stile, you will see the Obelisk and Stourhead House away
to your right but keep straight on, alongside the iron fence
and past the gates which cross the driveway, to a stile in the
corner of the fence. Over this stile, keep close to the wire
fence on your right and walk along the edge of the fine outer
garden of the summer house.

Over the next stile, you will be in a very large field but,
even if there are crops growing, the path will be clearly
marked ahead of you towards the cluster of buildings and the
twin-gabled farmhouse of "Home Farm". At the end of the
path, join the farm track around the edge of this unfenced
field and follow it, past the farmhouse, its boundary walls
and farm buildings, to the junction of tracks at a T-junction.
Turn left and follow the concrete track with a one-sided
avenue of beeches (if you can have a one-sided avenue) to the
end of the track. On the tarmac road, Stourton Lane, turn
right past the bus stop and walk down the road between hedges
and with a row of four cottages, built in 1941, on your left.

After a small copse, "Myrtle Tree Cottage" on the right and a
couple more cottages, the road turns left around Stourhead
park. Don't go left but go straight on through a wicket gate
onto the park track with an avenue of beech trees (both
sides). As the track bears right, prior to its long
anti-clockwise sweep to Stourhead House, the footpath goes off
as a straight line across the park to come out and join the
House drive after the House. However, you can stay on the
track and, through two iron gates in small iron-fenced
enclosures, you join the main gravel driveway near the House
with a wide grassy lawn on its left hand side.

Past the House, the drive swings round under a high bank of
rhododendrons and past the Gardens entrance and store yards on
the right. As the drive swings back the other way, there are
some really old, pollarded chestnut trees on the LH side where
the footpath comes back through the gate in the iron fence.

On down the drive, go through the stone gateway with a gatehouse on the left and turn down the high-banked lane on your right for tea, drinks or the church and Gardens. For collection, you could arrange for a car to meet you at the National Trust car park opposite or you could catch the bus at the bus shelter in Stourton - timetables permitting.

Before you leave Stourton - the Church of St Peter's dates from the 13th Century and parts of the original nave and tower still remain. Much rebuilding was carried out in the 16th Century and again after the Stourton estates were sold to the Hoare family in 1717. As usual, the Victorians carried out their own particular brand of restoration and, even as late as 1974, the old box pews were removed from the North aisle, the East end of which was made into a baptistry.

...join the main gravel driveway near
the House - Stourhead - Day 5, Page 137

Over the fence, you are in Six Wells Bottom
The source of the Stour - Day 5, Page 135

THE STOUR VALLEY PATH

IN CONCLUSION

How, in a few words, can the journey on foot from Mudeford
Quay to Six Wells Bottom be summarized adequately?

Everyone who has completed this Walk will bring away some
particular and lasting memory and each will have enjoyed a
certain Stage more than any other.

However, there has been so much variety encapsulated in this
Walk that we have seen a great deal of the delights of the
English countryside in a mere 60.1/2 miles. We have followed
the River Stour from its termination at the English Channel,
by the holiday conurbation of Christchurch and Bournemouth,
through rich arable and pasture land, past market towns and
mills, through villages and vales, all the way to its source
in the wooded valley of (and how English can you get?) Six
Wells Bottom.

Great houses, village churches and wayside inns have vied for
our attention whilst cattle and sheep have kept wary eyes on
us as we have traversed their home pastures. We have heard
village tales which have been handed down through generations
and we have heard a little of the history of some of the
villages through which we have walked but the best part of all
could not be described adequately in the written word. It is
just a feeling that, try as one might to avoid the expression,
we have been wrapped in "typically English" countryside - the
very essence of the England which haunts the memories and
dreams of many an expatriate Englishman and Englishwoman.

This has been a wander through William Barnes' country. It's
still here and he would surely still feel at home here even if
modern farming methods have brought superficial changes to the
landscape. It's still his "Blackwmore by the Stour" and I'm
certain that, as you've passed through some of the little
villages on your way, you will have passed cottages where,
just as in Barnes' day,

        "the maidens do stan' out in clusters avore
        the doors, vor to chatty an' zee vo'k goo by."

THE STOUR VALLEY PATH

ACKNOWLEDGMENTS

Preparation of "The Stour Valley Path" has involved many hours
of planning, poring over books, maps and timetables and
numerous visits to the County Library, Reference Department in
Bournemouth.

First of all, therefore, my thanks go to my wife, Janet, for
her forebearance during my long periods of pre-occupation and
for making sure that I never went out into the wilderness of
Dorset without adequate protection from the elements or from
the ravages of hunger.

Obviously, the Ordnance Survey maps to which reference is made
in the Introduction to this Walk are the major source of
information but, for historical information, I have to
acknowledge the immense work of the Rev John Hutchins'
"History and Antiquities of the County of Dorset" in four
volumes.

Secondly, the only other work to which much reference has been
made is a rare paperback of collected tales from Dorset
members of the Federation of Womens' Institutes which was
published before the outbreak of World War II.

Several works have appeared since then which carry exactly the
same tales of witches and ghosts, almost word for word, but
which have not offered acknowledgment to this book. However,
although this excellent little book is no longer available, I
would like to offer belated thanks to the Ladies of the
Institute who published "Dorset - Up Along and Down Along",
edited by Marianne R Dacombe (M.A.Oxon) and published by
D.F.W.I. way back in 1935.

INDEX

Tarrant Keynston Church,71

Tchertkov, Count,19

Tesco,21

Thorngrove,119

Throop Fisheries,21,25

Throop Mill,21,25,27

Throop Old Forge,25

Throop Weir,27

Todber,106

Tolstoy,19

Transport Connections,6

Transport, Rural Dorset,3,8

Uddens,43

Union Arms, Child Okeford,92

Upper Street,Ch Okeford,89,92

Upton Lane, Blandford,74,77

Valley Road, Throop,27

Vespasian,13,59

Vine House, Stur. Newton,97

Walnut Farm,57

Walnut Tree Farm,119

Walter de Eureux,49

Watch House,12

Waymarking/Signposting,4

West Street, Blandford,74

West Stour,109/10/11/13/14/16

West Stour Church, 116,117

Whistley House,124

Whistley Farm and Water,127

White Horse, Hinton St M.,102

Wick,14,16

Wight, Isle of,12,60

Wildlife/Countryside Act,4

William the Conqueror,43

Wilts/Dorset Buses,3,33,36,66

Wimborne Minster,3,51,57,60/6

Wimborne, Lady,50,51

Wimborne, St Cuthburga,57

Winterbourne Stickland,78

Wood Lane, Hinton St M.,102

Wyke,119,120,124

Wyke, Richard de,120

Yardgrove Farm,103,105

Yeomans Road, Throop,27

Zeals,129